Cheatin'

by Del Shores

A Samuel French Acting Edition

FOUNDED 1830
New York Hollywood London Toronto
SAMUELFRENCH.COM

Copyright © 1984 as "A Little Love, a Little Cheatin' & A Whole Lotta Somethin' Goin' On" by Del Shores
Copyright © 1991 as "Cheatin'" by Del Shores

ALL RIGHTS RESERVED

CAUTION: Professionals and amateurs are hereby warned that *CHEATIN'* is subject to a royalty. It is fully protected under the copyright laws of the United States of America, the British Commonwealth, including Canada, and all other countries of the Copyright Union. All rights, including professional, amateur, motion picture, recitation, lecturing, public reading, radio broadcasting, television and the rights of translation into foreign languages are strictly reserved. In its present form the play is dedicated to the reading public only.

The amateur live stage performance rights to *CHEATIN'* are controlled exclusively by Samuel French, Inc., and royalty arrangements and licenses must be secured well in advance of presentation. PLEASE NOTE that amateur royalty fees are set upon application in accordance with your producing circumstances. When applying for a royalty quotation and license please give us the number of performances intended, dates of production, your seating capacity and admission fee. Royalties are payable one week before the opening performance of the play to Samuel French, Inc., at 45 W. 25th Street, New York, NY 10010.

Royalty of the required amount must be paid whether the play is presented for charity or gain and whether or not admission is charged.

Stock royalty quoted upon application to Samuel French, Inc.

For all other rights than those stipulated above, apply to: Samuel French, Inc.

Particular emphasis is laid on the question of amateur or professional readings, permission and terms for which must be secured in writing from Samuel French, Inc.

Copying from this book in whole or in part is strictly forbidden by law, and the right of performance is not transferable.

Whenever the play is produced the following notice must appear on all programs, printing and advertising for the play: "Produced by special arrangement with Samuel French, Inc."

Due authorship credit must be given on all programs, printing and advertising for the play.

No one shall commit or authorize any act or omission by which the copyright of, or the right to copyright, this play may be impaired.
No one shall make any changes in this play for the purpose of production.
Publication of this play does not imply availability for performance. Both amateurs and professionals considering a production are strongly advised in their own interests to apply to Samuel French, Inc., for written permission before starting rehearsals, advertising, or booking a theatre.
No part of this book may be reproduced, stored in a retrieval system, or transmitted in any form, by any means, now known or yet to be invented, including mechanical, electronic, photocopying, recording, videotaping, or otherwise, without the prior written permission of the publisher.

ISBN 978-0-573-69302-1

For my Mom, Loraine

No one shall commit or authorize any act or omission by which the copyright of, or the right to copyright, this play may be impaired

No one shall make any changes in this play for the purpose of production

Publication of this play does not imply availability for performance Both amateurs and professionals considering a production are *strongly* advised in their own interests to apply to Samuel French, Inc , for written permission before starting rehearsals, advertising, or booking a theatre

No part of this book may be reproduced, stored in a retrieval system, or transmitted in any form, by any means, now known or yet to be invented, including mechanical, electronic, photocopying, recording, videotaping, or otherwise, without the prior written permission of the publisher

IMPORTANT BILLING AND CREDIT REQUIREMENTS

All producers of CHEATIN' *must* give credit to the Author of the Play in all programs distributed in connection with performances of the Play and in all instances in which the title of the Play appears for purposes of advertising, publicizing or otherwise exploiting the Play and/or a production The name of the Author *must* also appear on a separate line, on which no other name appears, immediately following the title, and *must* appear in size of type not less than fifty percent the size of the title type.

Cheatin' was originally produced by Rex Knowles for the Main Stage Theatre in North Hollywood, California October 18, 1984. The show then moved to the McCadden Place Theatre in Hollywood, CA to complete its run. It was directed by Sherry Landrum; the set was by William Maynard; the lights by Rex Knowles. The production stage managers were Addison Morgan and Kelley Alexander. The cast, in order of appearance, was as follows:

SID CRANFORD ....Newell Alexander

BO BOB JASPER............................. ....Earl Bullock

CLARENCE HOPKINS.......................................Del Shores

SARA LEE TURNOVER ....Gwen Harris

OVELLA PARSONS-WILKS ....Lana Schwab

TEDDY JOE WILKS ....Maxwell Morrow

MAYBELLINE CARTWRIGHT....................Patrika Darbo

Also appearing in various roles during the long run were: Addison Morgan, Noreen Reardon, Ernie Lively, Clark Nederjohn, Terry Brannon, Marilyn Hickey, Rosemary Alexander, and Sherry Landrum.

Cheatin' was originally produced in an Equity production by Richard Carrothers and Dennis D. Hennessy for Tiffany's Attic in Kansas City, Missouri. It was directed by James Assad; the scenic design was by Terry O'Reagan; lighting design was by Ruth Cain; costume design was by Willamina McCallum, sound design by Charlene Taylor; set contructions by James Design; set dressing by Ronald S. Freeby. The production stage manager was Kathy Stengel. The cast, in order of appearance, was as follows:

SID CRANFORD..Dan Putman

BO BOB JASPER ....Leslie Jordan

CLARENCE HOPKINS.......................................Del Shores

SARA LEE TURNOVER ....Janie Fopeano

OVELLA PARSONS-WILKS ....Starr Anderson

TEDDY JOE WILKS ....Craig Oldfather

MAYBELLINE CARTWRIGHT.....................Vicki Oleson

Cover Artwork by: Newell Alexander

SPECIAL THANKS TO:

Rev. & Mrs. W.D. Shores
James Bray

CHARACTERS

SID CRANFORD. The bar owner, psychic, storyteller. Older and wiser than the others.

BO BOB JASPER. The gullible, naive, dimwitted, postman.

CLARENCE HOPKINS. The smart-ass, womanizing mechanic.

SARA LEE TURNOVER. The confident, sassy, fun-loving beauty operator.

OVELLA PARSONS-WILKS. The town bitch.

TEDDY JOE WILKS. The handsome, athletic, cheated-on husband.

MAYBELLINE CARTWRIGHT. The overweight, love-hungry, gossipy waitress.

PRODUCTION NOTE

The production of *Cheatin'* at the Main Stage Theatre was staged in a manner where there were only two blackouts—one at the end of the first act and one at the end of the play. The scenes overlapped (as indicated in the script), so the play moved at a rapid pace. To facilitate the overlapping, the bed in the Lowake Inn was positioned with the headboard downstage, allowing the actors to enter the Lowake Inn without being seen by the audience when necessary. Also, the mirror in the Oui Coiffer was imaginary, facing the audience.

PROLOGUE

Bluebell's.
SID comes through the front door of Bluebell's, coffee in
hand, begins to open up the bar, and addresses the
audience.

SID. Well, howdy. My name's Sid. Sid Cranford. I wanna welcome yew to my bar and dinin' facility—Bluebell's. Bluebell's Bar—and Dinin' Facility. It's mostly a bar though. Even though we do serve up a damn good bowl o' chili. And the cornbread ain't bad. But it's mostly a bar. So sit right down. Relax. Take a load off. And enjoy. I know I'm goin' to. (*Picks up his guitar.*) I'm a sanger, and a songwriter, bar owner, and psychic. Some people sez I oughta be in the Grand Ol' Opery—but hell, I don't know. I'll let ya'll decide. Be kind now. Yew know what the Good Book sez. (*Sings* Cheatin' *[music at back of script], after clapping begins.*) Thank yew. Thank yew. (*Every bit the star.*) Yure so kind. Yure ever so kind. Wrote that 'un myself. I write a lotta songs. Jest take real life situations and put music to 'em. Jest like Willie and Waylon and the boys. That there song was inspired by a few of our more prominent citizens right here in the town of Lowake. Yew'd be surprised at what goes on here in Lowake. Yew wud. Them soap operys ain't got nothin' on these folks. And yew know, to the untrained eye, Lowake's jest a little borin', do-nuthin', one-horse town. Not many folks visit Lowake either, unless they take a wrong turn—but now and then, we git 'em wanderin' in here jest lost as a whore in church. I love out-a-staters myself. All prissy-assed with their high-falutin' accents. They come in here and say, "Sir, where are we? We seem to have lost our way." And I always say, "Yure smack dab in the middle of Lowake, Texas." And they say, "Lowake? Where is that in relationship to a major city?" And I always say, "Well, it's jest North of Rowena, Southeast a Veribest, jest Northwest a Ballinger, in Concho County." (*Whoopin' it up.*) Shit—that always gits their goat. (*To himself.*) Major city, my ass. (*Thinking.*) Now where was I? Oh yeah, I was tellin' yew about the folks here in Lowake. (*Very sincere and hush-hush.*) Somethin' happened in our little town, and well, I jest don't want ta see enybody git hurt, that's all. 'Cause it ain't over yet. It all started on what seemed like jest a regular ol' day, jest like today. I opened Bluebell's here and jest like ever'day, our local mailman, Bo Bob Jasper, walked right through the door.

(*BO BOB enters, takes his cap off and puts it on the hat stand and goes to the table to sit.*)

BO BOB. Mornin', Sid, nice day, ain't it?
SID. An' that's where my story begins...

ACT I

Scene 1

*Bluebell's
The scene continues.*

SID. Mornin' Bo Bob. Yeah, real nice.

(BO BOB starts sorting his mail on the table while SID continues to the audience.)

SID. Bo Bob's our local mailman.

(BO BOB is having trouble deciding on which stacks to put each piece of mail.)

SID. He comes in here ever' mornin' to sort his mail. Bo Bob is the most moral, upright, human bein' in the whole state a Texas. He don't drank, he don't smoke, he don't cuss and he don't fool around—even though he ain't married. Accordin' to most folks, he also don't have a helluva lot o' fun either. And he's kinda dumb. He mostly jest comes in here to Bluebell's jest to jaw—and he always orders a root beer.

BO BOB. Can I have a root beer, Sid?

SID. Comin' right up, Bo Bob. *(HE gets a root beer, gives it to Bo Bob as HE continues to talk.)* If I 'member right, they kept 'im back onced in grade school. My mama always sed that Bo Bob wasn't right bright. But sometimes, I thank he's got more on the ball than folks give 'im credit for. But I do admit—his porch light is flickerin' a bit.

(BO BOB has finished sorting his mail in neat piles, then knocks it all on the floor when HE goes for his root beer.)

SID. Knocks that mail off ever' damn day.
CLARENCE. *(Entering)* Mornin', Sid. Mornin', Bo Bob.
SID & BO BOB. Mornin', Clarence.
CLARENCE. *(Snickering)* Yew still havin' problems sortin' that mail are ya, Bo Bob?
BO BOB. Yeah, wanna give me a hand?
CLARENCE. Sure. *(Picks up one piece)* Gimme a Lone Star, Sid. I gotta git my daily dose a vitamins.

(SID complies, CLARENCE downs the beer)

SID. *(Continuing to audience, as BO BOB continues to pick up and sort the mail.)* Believe it or not, Clarence and Bo Bob there are best friends. Clarence runs Hopkins Brothers up the street. People sez that him and his brother Otis are the best mechanics in West Texas. Otis ain't in this story. People come as far as Ballinger, Winters, and San Angelo to have the Hopkins boys work on their cars.

(CLARENCE catches a glimpse of himself in the mirror behind the bar.)

SID. Now Clarence is what some folks would call a ladies' man. Myself—I just thank he's a perty good ol' boy who has been blessed with that certain somethin' that the women go for. He ain't a perty boy—but he shore has somethin'.

CLARENCE. (*As HE exits.*) I gotta git to work. Take it easy, Sid. Or take it eny way yew can git it. (*Slaps Bo Bob on the back, laughing at his own joke.*)

SID. See ya, Clarence.

(*SARA LEE enters as CLARENCE exits and THEY ad-lib exchanges. THEY kiss passionately.*)

SID. (*To audience.*) Now Clarence has been datin' Sara Lee Turnover since they was all kids.

(*CLARENCE exits.*)

SARA LEE. Gawd I love a man in a uniform. Mornin', Sid. Hey, Bo Bob. Is that my Cosmo?

BO BOB. (*Checking to make sure.*) Sure is.

SARA LEE. Hey, Sid, yew got eny a them fried pies? I got me a cravin' for a cherry 'un.

SID. Jest got in a new batch this mornin'. Help yureself. My waitress is late as usual. Jest leave a quarter on the counter.

(*SARA LEE finds the pies and starts eating and reading her Cosmo.*)

SID. Now, Sara Lee runs the beauty shop—the Oui Coiffer [pronounced co-eee-fer]—that sets across the street from Bluebell's and right down from the Hopkins Brothers. Shoo-wee—it took ol' Sara Lee years to teach us how to pronounce the name of 'er damn ol' beauty shop. Some of 'em still ain't got it right. It's a French word, ya know.

(SARA LEE is now changing her hair style in the mirror over the bar, according to a Cosmo ad.)

SID. Now I've been told that Clarence and Sara Lee git it on nearly ever' day, on the linoleum of 'er shop, mind yew, during their lunch hour. Well, that's what I been told.

SARA LEE. *(Looking at watch and exiting.)* Ooh—I gotta go. That was a mighty fine fried pie.

SID. *(Looking after Sara Lee)* I'd love to sample 'em myself sometime. *(To audience.)* What a sweetie pie. I shore did envy that Clarence Hopkins. Ever' man in town did. And for the life a me, I never understood why he messed around on Sara Lee with Ovella Parsons—I mean, Wilks. He was jugglin' two women, one of 'em married and that Ovella is a bitch on wheels if I ever saw one.

OVELLA. *(Storms into Bluebells)* Sid, have yew seen that sorry, no count husband a mine?

SID. No I haven't—and good mornin' to yew too, Ovella.

OVELLA. *(Has found the fried pies.)* Are these fried pies fresh?

SID. Yes, ma'am. Help yureself. Jest got 'em in this mornin'.

(OVELLA proceeds to eat one bite, doesn't like it and throws is back into the container of fresh ones)

SID. Ovella is still perty damn good lookin' and look at all that perty hair. (*Shakes head*) Hmph.

(*OVELLA spots the mirror and begins primping.*)

SID. She was head cheerleader, homecomin' queen and football sweetheart in high school. All the boys loved 'er. All the gals hated 'er guts. Especially Sara Lee Turnover.

SARA LEE. (*Reenters Bluebell's.*) Oh, Sid, I fergot to pay. (*SHE spots Ovella*) Mornin', Ovella.

OVELLA. Mornin', Sara Lee.

SARA LEE & OVELLA. (*Turning away from one another.*) Bitch.

SARA LEE. That sure was a good fried pie, Sid. Here's yure quarter.

SID. Thanks, sweetie.

(*SARA LEE exits.*)

OVELLA. I hope yew don't expect me to pay for these. Yew can git rocks free out in the parkin' lot.

(*SHE exits and upon doing so, knocks Bo Bob's mail off, and picks it up, with her butt right in his face; BO BOB reacts.*)

SID. Good to see yew too, Ovella. Now Ovella's husband is Teddy Joe Wilks. Ovella and Teddy Joe were in a few folks eyes Mr. and Mrs. Perfect Couple. In other words, they looked good together—'cause they fought like cats and dawgs.

TEDDY JOE. (*Enters and calls out after Ovella.*) Yeah, well, why don't yew plan on stayin' home tonight and cook me some supper? I'm as hungry as a big ol' bear. It's a wifely duty to fix her husband breakfast, yew know. (*HE jogs in wearing exercise clothes.*)

OVELLA. (*Offstage.*) Aw, stick it in the microwave.

TEDDY JOE. Mornin', Sid. Mornin', Bo Bob. Yew got enythang to eat, Sid? Ovella didn't fix no breakfast agin.

SID. Help yureself to one of them fresh fried pies.

TEDDY JOE. Thanks, could yew heat it up for me? And I'll take a Lone Star.

BO BOB. Mornin', Teddy Joe. Nice day, ain't it?

TEDDY JOE. Sure is.

BO BOB. (*Hands Teddy Joe a* Playboy Magazine.) Here's yure smut magazine ... and Orvella was lookin' for yew. (*Name is intentionally mispronounced.*)

TEDDY JOE. (*Opening* Playboy *to the centerfold.*) Yeah? Well, she can jest go to hell, Bo Bob. (*HE stretches some.*)

SID. Teddy Joe sells insurance down at Lloyds and keeps in shape. He runs three miles a day—at least that's what he claims. And he works out with weights in his garage to this very day. He was a perty good quarterback in high school.

(*MAYBELLINE rushes in to Bluebell's with her hair in curlers.*)

MAYBELLINE. Sorry I'm late agin, cousin Sid. I had car trouble and that Clarence Hopkins was givin' me a hard time. He shore is cute, though. (*SHE has already moved in on the fried pies and proceeds to eat one.*) Hi, Bo

Bob. Hey, Teddy Joe. How's yure lovely wife?

TEDDY JOE. Fine, jest fine, Maybelline.

BO BOB. (*A little shy.*) Hi, Maybelline.

SID. Them fried pies is fresh, Maybelline. Help yureself.

MAYBELLINE. (*Mouth full*) Thanks, Sid.

SID. (*To audience.*) Maybelline's my first cousin on my mama's side. She's a Cartwright and she's Sara Lee's best friend. As yew've probably realized, she's my waitress here. Been workin' for me about three weeks. Longest she's ever held a job. Had to give it to 'er. Family pressures. She got fired ever' where else in town—the Dairy Queen, the bank, Lloyds, Rocket Gas ...

MAYBELLINE. Can I have a bag of Fritos, Sid? Didn't have time for breakfast. (*Not missing a beat, takes a bag and begins to eat.*) I giss ya'll heard about the Barnes. They're gettin' a divorce after twenty-four years a marriage. I jest cain't believe it. It's the biggest mess I ever seen in my life. I thought they was so happy together ... (*SHE exits shaking her head, into the back room, comes back still eating, with a broom and starts sweeping.*)

SID. Maybelline gits the dirt on ever'one in town 'cause she's a gossip. If yew want to know enythang about enybody in Concho County, then ask ol' Maybellıne. Stickin' that nose into every'one else's bees wax. (*Sympathetic.*) Poor baby. Never had a date in her life.

(*MAYBELLINE is staring at Bo Bob as SHE sweeps*)

SID. She has a weight problem. Truth is, she's jest flat out fat. But Maybellıne figures pretty big, no pun intended, in this story. Well, thangs are about to happen ... wait a second. (*Holds head.*) Before they do, I'm gittin' one of my psychic feelin's. (*Back to audience.*) Yew know, I git it from my grandmammy, Bertha Cranford. She was a psychic healer. She could stop bleedin' from five miles away. (*Holds his head again.*) Oh, yeah ... this is a big 'un. It's a prediction. (*Releases his head.*) I predict that the Dallas Cowboys are gonna kick the L.A. Rams' asses back to by gawd Disneyland where they belong. And remember, yew heard it from Sid. Sid Cranford.

TEDDY JOE. So, Bo Bob. What's cookin'?

BO BOB. (*Sniffs*) I don't know. I don't smell nothin'.

MAYBELLINE. Cousin Sid, can I have the day off so I can go over to Sara Lee's to git my hair combed out? She sed she could fit me in between Ovella Parsons—I mean Wilks—and Clara Bell Ivey. Please, can I, Sid?

SID. Okay, honey, but yure gonna have ta make it up by takin' inventory next week.

MAYBELLINE. I will, I promise. Thanks a million.

(*SHE rushes out, SID shakes his head.*)

TEDDY JOE. So, Bo Bob, what's cookin'?

BO BOB. Maybe it's them fried pies.

TEDDY JOE. I mean—what's going on, Bo Bob? What's happenin' in yure life?

BO BOB. Oh, I git it. It's like that Hank Williams song, "Hey good lookin', whatcha got cookin'?" For the longest time I used to thank that was a song about a girl invitin' a boy over for supper. Then Clarence explained it to me.

TEDDY JOE. Well, I'm glad that yew got that figured out so's that life can go on.

BO BOB. Well, yew know Clarence. Smart as a whip.

CHEATIN' 19

He can take an engine apart and put it back together blindfolded.

TEDDY JOE. I'm so jealous I cain't hardly stand it.

BO BOB. Me, too. But yew ain't got no reason to be jealous, Teddy Joe. Yew probably make more money than enybody in this town. A big successful insurance salesman wearin' a three-piece suit. Heck—I'm jealous of yew.

TEDDY JOE. Of me? Aw, come on, Bo Bob. Yew got a good job, too. And that uniform ain't so bad.

BO BOB. We're gettin' short britches this summer.

TEDDY JOE. See there.

BO BOB. Yeah—but yew and Clarence have somethin' special. It takes talent to do what yew two do. Enybody can deliver mail. (*Takes a card out of the bag and goes through the motions.*) All ya do is drop it in the box and go to the next 'un. And if there's a red flag up, yew take the out goin' mail and put it right here. (*Indicates.*) Or sometimes, yew go in a business and say, "Here's yure mail, Mr. or Mrs. so-an-so." (*HE hands the card he is demonstrating with to Teddy Joe.*) And that's it.

(*TEDDY JOE reads the outside of the card and something is wrong.*)

BO BOB. What's the matter, Teddy Joe?

TEDDY JOE. Where did yew git this card, Bo Bob?

BO BOB. At the post office. That's where I pick up all my mail.

TEDDY JOE. This card is addressed to Clarence Hopkins. Do yew know who it's from, Bo Bob?

BO BOB. (*Trying to take the letter, TEDDY JOE not letting him.*) Let me see it. Usually the person who sent it puts their name and address in the corner up there ...

TEDDY JOE. I know letter writin' procedures, Bo Bob. This 'un dudn't have a return address though. (*Shows the letter at arms length.*) Do yew recoginize that handwritin', Bo Bob?

BO BOB. (*Lying.*) Well, no, Teddy Joe. I cain't say that I do. It's real perty though.

TEDDY JOE. That's my wife's handwritin', Bo Bob. Now why would my wife be writing' to Clarence Hopkins?

BO BOB. Maybe she's havin' car trouble, Teddy Joe.

TEDDY JOE. The car's runnin' fine, Bo Bob. I thank yew know somethin' yew ain't tellin'. And I thank yew better start tellin'.

BO BOB. I don't know nuthin', Teddy Joe.

TEDDY JOE. Ain't that the truth. Yew ain't got the brains God gave a piss-ant.

BO BOB. That wadn't very nice, Teddy Joe.

TEDDY JOE. Naw, it wadn't, was it? Well, I'll tell yew what will be nice. It'll be nice to find out what this here card sez.

BO BOB. I cain't let yew do that, Teddy Joe. That's against the law.

TEDDY JOE. Oh, it is? Well, what are yew gonna do about it, Mr. Mailman, make a citizen's arrest?

BO BOB. I jest may have to do that, Teddy Joe.

TEDDY JOE. (*Opens the card, takes it out.*) Well, as yew can see, I'm scered shitless. (*HE reads it.*)

BO BOB. Teddy Joe, yew shouldn'ta dun that.

TEDDY JOE. (*Pause.*) I think yew may be right this time, Bo Bob. The Lowake Inn, huh?

(*LIGHTS come up in the Lowake Inn. OVELLA and*

*CLARENCE are laughing. CLARENCE lights a
cigarette.)*

TEDDY JOE. (*Reading.*) "Happy Anniversary to the man that makes me happy. P.S. And horny."
BO BOB. (*Puzzled.*) Horny?
TEDDY JOE. (*Still reading*) "See yew agin at ten o'clock on Monday at the Lowake Inn." (*Muttering*) Happy Anniversary? Must of been goin' on awhile. And I giss yew knew about this all along, Bo Bob? (*Yelling.*) Did yew, Bo Bob?
BO BOB. Well, no. I don't know. I jest ...

(TEDDY JOE grabs him by the collar.)

BO BOB. Yeah, I did!
TEDDY JOE. (*Looks at watch*) Well, it's ten-fifteen—I think I got some bizness to take care of at the Lowake Inn. (*To Bo Bob*) Some friend yew've turned out to be. (*HE storms out of Bluebell's*)
BO BOB. Well, Clarence is my friend, too. (*Frustrated*) Durn it all. I hate this. (*HE exits*)

*(SID exits into his stock room as LIGHTS go down in
  Bluebell's.)*

ACT I

Scene 2

The Lowake Inn
Full LIGHTS come up.
CLARENCE and OVELLA are in bed, having just made
   love.

CLARENCE. What say we go at it agin, Ovella?
OVELLA. Good Lord, Clarence. What are yew? Some kinda sex machine?
CLARENCE. Yew bet your little bohuncus I am. And as far as I've been able to tell, yew are, too.
OVELLA. Happy Anniversary, Clarence. (*Kissing him madly, passionately.*)
CLARENCE. Happy Anniversary, baby.
OVELLA. You make me a maniac, Clarence. The feelin's yew stir up within my soul are pert near out of this world.

(THEY continue dialogue as THEY kiss.)

CLARENCE. Heavenly?
OVELLA. In a sinful sort of way.
CLARENCE. Well, yew know what the song sez. "Heaven's jest a sin away."
OVELLA. (*Off key.*) "Wo, wo, just a sin away."
CLARENCE. Gawd, I love the way you sang.
OVELLA. Clarence?
CLARENCE. What?
OVELLA. Nuthin'. I was jest sayin' yure name as the

CHEATIN' 23

passion was a mountin'.

CLARENCE. Well, let it mount.

(THEY've finished kissing, SHE looks at the tattoo on his chest, a big eagle.)

OVELLA. God, I love that tattoo!

CLARENCE. Wanna' see it fly? *(HE moves his chest and arms to accommodate.)* They do 'em up right in the Navy, don't they?

OVELLA. *(Kissing the tattoo)* They shore do. Teddy Joe was in the Army, yew know. He never got a tattoo. But he was a hell of a quarterback in high school.

CLARENCE. Would that be the quarterback for the same team that got its butt kicked by ever' one in our district except the Ballinger B team?

OVELLA. The very. Oh, Clarence, yew are so funny. I jest love a man with a sense of humor.

CLARENCE. Well, I can crack a perty damn good joke.

OVELLA. Tell me one. *(Looking at watch)* But hurry up. I gotta git home and cook Teddy Joe's supper.

CLARENCE. Okay. Why don't Baptists make love standin' up?

OVELLA. *(Laughing)* Oh, I can tell this 'un's gonna be a good 'un. Why, Clarence, why?

CLARENCE. Because they're scered the Methodists will thank they're dancin'.

OVELLA. *(As THEY whoop it up.)* Oh, that is nasty, Clarence. Yew tell the best jokes. I swear yew do.

(An ENGINE roars outside.)

OVELLA. Did yew hear that?

CLARENCE. What? What was that? (*Continues kissing Ovella as the ENGINE roars louder.*)

OVELLA. Clarence, that's Teddy Joe's pickup!

CLARENCE. Well, it needs a tune-up.

OVELLA. Oh, my God! What are we gonna do? Git under the bed, Clarence! Hurry!

CLARENCE. I ain't gittin' under no dirty-ass bed. Jest calm down, Ovella. He'll probably go away. We mustn't panic.

OVELLA. We mustn't panic?!! My husband is out in the parkin' lot of the Lowake Inn, sportin' his big ol' arm muscles—I'm in here with the local mechanic, both of us in our underwear, and yew tell me not to panic?! (*Beat.*) God, Clarence, I wish yew'd start wearin' regular shorts, them ol' boxers are just gawd-awful. (*SHE moves to the window and peeks out.*)

CLARENCE. Well, Sara Lee happens to like 'em.

(*LIGHTS start to come up in the Out Coiffer. SARA LEE enters.*)

OVELLA. Oh my gawd, Clarence. Teddy Joe's takin' down that double-barrel shotgun from the gun rack behind the seat of his pick-up truck.

CLARENCE. (*Calmly*) Ovella. (*Hysterically*) Now we can panic!

(*CLARENCE and OVELLA scramble for their clothes and exit into the bathroom as LIGHTS go down.*)

ACT I

Scene 3

Oui Coiffer Salon
Full LIGHTS come up as SARA LEE sits down and reads her "Cosmo," then primps in the mirror a little, touches up her hair as MAYBELLINE rushes into the Oui Coiffer.

MAYBELLINE. Sorry I'm late, Sara Lee. I took the curlers out.

SARA LEE. Yure gonna be late to yure own funeral, honey. How are thangs down at Bluebell's?

MAYBELLINE. Fine. I thank I'm gonna git to keep this job.

SARA LEE. Yew'd better. Yure runnin' outta places to work. *(SHE starts spraying Maybelline's hair.)* And I don't need a manicurist.

MAYBELLINE. Watch it! Yure gettin' it in my eyes!

SARA LEE. Well, hold still and that won't happen. I am a highly trained professional, Maybelline.

MAYBELLINE. I realize that, Sara Lee, but yew do make mistakes occasionally, too, don't yew?

SARA LEE. Rarely. *(SHE finishes the spraying.)* Now, we'll let it set a spell and then I'll comb it out. *(Lighting a cigarette.)* You know, Maybelline—I think you ought to take up smokin'. Men really go for it, and Lord knows, it curbs the appetite.

MAYBELLINE. Men go for it? I didn't know that!

SARA LEE. Well, honey—Where do yew live? Podunk, Texas? Of course men go for it. Clarence loves me to smoke. That's why I took it up.

MAYBELLINE. Well, I don't want to get cancer. I jest don't know.

SARA LEE. Aw, hells bells, Maybelline. My grandpa Merck lived to be a hunderdt and three and he smoked four packs of cigarettes ever' day of his life. All that surgeon general stuff is a buncha hawg-wash. Now, give me that glass over there. *(MAYBELLINE does.)* This here's a martini. *(SHE takes a drag from the cigarette, then sips from the glass; SHE lowers her voice)* Well, hello there, care to join me for a drank?

MAYBELLINE. Oh, that is sexy, Sara Lee. Let me try it.

SARA LEE. Okay, here yew go. *(SHE hands her the cigarette.)*

MAYBELLINE. *(Strikes a pose, then takes a puff.)* Well, hello ... *(Coughs her head off.)* Oh, my gawd! I thank I'm gonna die. *(Gives her back the cigarette.)* Here, I don't want it.

SARA LEE. I'll teach yew to French inhale after I comb this out. Now yew work on drankin' that there martini while I comb yew out. *(MAYBELLINE does.)* Now hold yure little fanger out—that's right. Men love that. And Maybelline, don't ever agin order a beer in front of men—unless yew really know him, like me and Clarence.

MAYBELLINE. *(Looking at herself in the mirror as Sara Lee continues to do her hair.)* I jest don't know, Sara Lee. I jest don't know.

SARA LEE. And what is it, honey, that yew jest don't know this time?

MAYBELLINE. I jest don't know if this is gonna work.

SARA LEE. Maybelline, yew do know that yew are tryin' my patience. Now yew gotta trust me, sugar, or yure gonna get me all riled up and yure hair ain't gonna turn out worth a flyin' flit.

MAYBELLINE. Okay, Sara Lee, I trust yew. But if this don't get me a date, I'm gonna give up.

SARA LEE. Turn to page seventy-three in that magazine.

MAYBELLINE. (*Turns to the page*) Okay.

SARA LEE. Now what do you see?

MAYBELLINE. Some ol' homely girl. Ugly as homemade sin. Looks like Wilma Burns in high school. The child ain't got no eyebrows.

SARA LEE. Oh, Wilma Burns. Gawd she was ugly. She could bite a hawg through a picket fence. I wonder whatever happened to her?

MAYBELLINE. She got knocked up by Clement Barnes. They're livin' over in Abilene. Got three kids and one in the oven.

SARA LEE. I'd hate to see them kids.

SARA LEE & MAYBELLINE. (*Together.*) Uggglly!

SARA LEE. Buck teeth and no eyebrows. Now, do yew consider yureself pertier or uglier than that Wilma Burns look-a-like?

MAYBELLINE. With or without makeup?

SARA LEE. (*Losing patience*) Without I giss. It don't look like she's wearin' eny to me.

MAYBELLINE. (*Pondering.*) Well, she's skinny as an ol' bean-pole, Sara Lee, but other than that, I giss we're about even.

SARA LEE. Okay, flip the page.

MAYBELLINE. Well, help-me-Hanna! Is this the same girl?

SARA LEE. The very.

MAYBELLINE. This is unbelievable. Pure-dee unbelievable. Am I gonna look that good?

SARA LEE. Better. (*SHE finishes her hair. It is a wild, unruly looking style, like only the models in fashion magazines can get away with.*) Well, what do you thank?

MAYBELLINE. Yure through?

SARA LEE. Yeah, ain't it gorgeous?

MAYBELLINE. Well, I don't know, Sara Lee.

SARA LEE. What do yew mean, yew don't know?

MAYBELLINE. Oh, I don't know. I jest feel kinda silly.

SARA LEE. Maybelline, Cher wore this very doo on the Academy Awards two years ago.

MAYBELLINE. And it's still in style?

SARA LEE. It's jest now gettin' down here to Lowake. And now for your lashes.

MAYBELLINE. Now, don't overdo it. I don't want to look like some two-bit whore.

SARA LEE. Trust me, Maybelline, trust me. (*SARA LEE proceeds to give Maybelline the full make-up treatment, including false eyelashes.*)

MAYBELLINE. Okay. (*Pause.*) I shore do hate my name. Maybe if I changed my name, I'd get more dates.

SARA LEE. Well, quite frankly, I don't think that's the problem. I hate my name too, and as yew well know, I have no problem gittin' dates.

MAYBELLINE. What's wrong with yure name? I like yure name.

SARA LEE. Sara Lee. Shit. Mama thought it'd be so cute to have a little girl named Sara Lee Turnover. How'd yew like to be named after a fried pie?

MAYBELLINE. Well, it's better than Maybelline Cartwright. What about Mitzi—or Tiffany—or Crystal! Crystal Cartwright!

SARA LEE. Don't be so negative. That's why yew don't get eny dates. I bet that Bo Bob Jasper would ask yew out in a heartbeat if yew wadn't so negative.

MAYBELLINE. (*Sighs.*) Bo Bob Jasper would? (*Beat*) What about Clarence Hopkins?

SARA LEE. I'm ignorin' that comment, Miz Maybelline.

MAYBELLINE. (*Sinking in.*) Too negative, huh?

SARA LEE. That's right. Yure a damn pessimist. I, on the other hand, am a optimist—a positive thanker. (*SHE has finished the make-up and turns Maybelline to the mirror.*)

MAYBELLINE. (*Looks, then*) Well, there's one thang I am positive of...

SARA LEE. And what's that, sugar?

MAYBELLINE. I do look like a two-bit whore.

(*LIGHTS start to come up in the Lowake Inn as OVELLA comes out of the bathroom dressed*)

SARA LEE. Well, they git dates, don't they?

MAYBELLINE. Yes, I giss they do. (*All excited*) I gotta go. I gotta find me some clothes to go with this new doo. See ya, Sara Lee. And thanks.

SARA LEE. Good luck!

(MAYBELLINE exits out the front door and SARA LEE exits into the back of the Oui Coiffer as the LIGHTS go down.)

ACT I

Scene 4

The Lowake Inn.
Full LIGHTS come up.
Offstage TEDDY JOE is KNOCKING at the door. The KNOCKS become POUNDS. OVELLA frantically straightens up the room.

TEDDY JOE. (*Offstage.*) Open up, Ovella. I mean it!

(OVELLA opens the door as TEDDY JOE bursts in with his shotgun, SHE throws her arms around him.)

OVELLA. Hello, pumpkin bear. How's ...
TEDDY JOE. (*Pushing her aside.*) Where is that low-down, mangy hound dawg, Clarence Hopkins?
OVELLA. (*Prying the shotgun away from Teddy Joe.*) Oh, Teddy Joe, yew are so funny. I jest love a man with a sense of humor. (*SHE puts the shotgun behind her.*)
TEDDY JOE. Ovella, quit playin' games with me. (*Looking around.*) Did he crawl out the winda?
OVELLA. (*Throwing her arms around Teddy Joe.*) Teddy Joe, honey—I don't know what yure so fired up about. I giss yew didn't git my note.

TEDDY JOE. *(Playing along.)* What note?

OVELLA. The note that told yew to meet me here. I left it on the kitchen table, pumpkin bear. Yew see ... the other day I was watchin' Dr. Ruth and her topic of the day was ... "How to Add a Spark to an Otherwise Dull Married Sex Life." And one idea was to meet yure spouse at a motel, watch dirty movies, and act like teenagers on the make agin. Well, the Lowake Inn don't have no dirty movies, but we'll make do. Yew did git the note, Teddy Joe?

TEDDY JOE. Ovella, yure lyin' to me.

OVELLA. Have I ever lied to my sweet pumpkin bear?

TEDDY JOE. Hell yeah, yew have.

OVELLA. Well, okay. So I've lied. But not a big whopper like this one ... I mean, like this one yure accusin' me of. *(Starts to cry)* I'm hurt, Teddy Joe. I thought there was more to our marriage than this. I thought yew trusted me.

TEDDY JOE. Well, what gave yew that idea?

OVELLA. What do I have to do, swear on Gideon's Bible? *(SHE puts her hand on the Bible.)*

TEDDY JOE. I wudn't do that if I was yew, Ovella. Now, where is that lousy son-of-a-... Where is he?

(OVELLA starts to panic, crying louder than ever in an effort to distract Teddy Joe from his search.)

TEDDY JOE. Now hush up, Ovella. That ain't gonna change my mind. I'm gonna find that buzzard, beat the shit outta him, then I'll deal with yew later.

OVELLA. I want a divorce, Teddy Joe! There's absolutely no use in us stayin' married if yew don't trust me.

TEDDY JOE. Well, then, we've got us a little problem here. 'Cause I sure as hell don't trust yew, and I ain't givin' yew no divorce jest sos yew and Clarence can shack up.

OVELLA. Then how about a trial separation? It worked for Dave and Penny on "Search For Another World."

TEDDY JOE. This is real life, Ovella. Not some stupid-ass soap opery. Now, where is that sorry son-of-a ...

OVELLA. (*Taking the shotgun and her handbag as SHE starts to exit.*) Clarence is not here, Teddy Joe. And there is nothin' goin' on between the two of us. I don't know where yew got that idea, but obviously yure havin' a whale of a good time actin' like some kinda lunatic. This is it, Teddy Joe! I'm leavin' yew for good. Yure as crazy as Bo Bob Jasper.

(*LIGHTS start to come up in the Oui Coiffer as BO BOB enters.*)

BO BOB. Mail deliv'ry.

OVELLA. (*Still gathering things to leave.*) They'll be shippin' yew off to Big Sprangs before the week is up. Goodbye! (*SHE storms out the door.*)

TEDDY JOE. (*À la Marlon Brando.*) Ovella! Ovella! (*HE knowingly exits in the bathroom to find CLARENCE as the LIGHTS go down.*)

ACT I

Scene 5

Oui Coiffer Salon.
Full LIGHTS come up, and ...
SARA LEE comes out of the back BO BOB is admiring himself in the mirror.

SARA LEE. Mornin', Bo Bob.

BO BOB. (*Almost jumping out of his skin.*) Mail Deliv'ry!

SARA LEE. Bo Bob, what a delight it is to see yew today.

BO BOB. It is?

SARA LEE. Why yes. It is. Yew always brighten up ol' Sara Lee's day with that great big grin of yures and all that important mail—and yew know how I jest love a man in uniform.

BO BOB. Well, good-niss, Sara Lee. I never knew. We're a gittin' new uniforms this summer. (*Laughs*) Git this—we even have the choice of wearin' short britches. Can yew believe it? Short britches on a U.S. of A. mailman.

SARA LEE. I thank that yew'd look kinda sexy in short britches, Bo Bob. I'm gettin' goose bumps jest imaginin' yew in short britches. (*Holds out her arm*) Feel.

BO BOB. (*HE does.*) Well, durn-it-all, yew shore are. Look at them little critters. I jest always had it in my mind that it'd kinda look sissified to wear short britches.

SARA LEE. Not true, Bo Bob. The very opposite. With those masculine legs of yures and that masculine body ...

(*Shivers.*) Ooooooh! I cain't stand it. Change the subject, quick!

BO BOB. (*Without missing a beat.*) Mrs. Annie Sue Langford didn't get any mail today. She was real upset. Turned on me like a mother-in-law. Thought her Social Security check would come in. And come to think of it, it usually does come in on the first Monday of the month. Mr. Barnes, on the other hand, got his ...

SARA LEE. That's enough, Bo Bob. That did it. I done come down off a my enormous high. See ... no more goose bumps. Yew ladies' man, yew.

BO BOB. Aw, come on, Sara Lee. Yew know that ain't true.

SARA LEE. The hell it ain't. Listen, Bo Bob. I hear it ever' day. Yes sir, ever' day a different woman's tellin' me about her fantasies with Bo Bob Jasper, that sexy mailman. And some of 'em git perty durn raunchy.

BO BOB. Yure teasin' me, Sara Lee.

SARA LEE. I am not, Bo Bob. Just trust ol' Sara Lee, will yew? Yesterday, it was Clara Bell Ivey.

BO BOB. (*In disbelief.*) Clara Bell Ivey?

SARA LEE. Said that yew come to deliver her mail, bent over to pet ol' Sam, that ugly mutt of hers, and she got a hot flash jest lookin' at yure sexy bohind. (*SHE slaps him on the butt.*)

BO BOB. Sara Lee!

SARA LEE. I swear on my mama's grave, it's true. And today, a single young voluptuous woman was gettin' all gussied up jest in case she ran into you.

(*LIGHTS start to come up in Bluebell's as MAYBELLINE enters wearing a mini dress, boa, high heels and can barely walk. SHE goes and sits at the bar.)*

BO BOB. Who?
SARA LEE. I ain't tellin'. I promised, and Sara Lee don't break her promises.
BO BOB. C'mon, Sara Lee. Tell me.
SARA LEE. Nuh-uh. I won't do it. But I will tell yew this. She's sittin' this very minute in Bluebell's drankin' a martini, jest waitin' for the right man to sweep her off her feet.

(One of Maybelline's lashes comes off SHE reacts and exits into the bathroom.)

BO BOB. Really?
SARA LEE. Really. So, why don't yew go down there and do some sweepin'?
BO BOB. I cain't Sara Lee. I just cain't.
SARA LEE. Cain't never did do enythang. Why not?
BO BOB. I don't know. I jest cain't. Yew know ...
SARA LEE. No, I do not know. And I ain't no good at suspense. Yew can trust ol' Sara Lee, Bo Bob.
BO BOB. Can yew keep a secret?
SARA LEE. Does ol' lady Barnes have varicose veins?
BO BOB. Promise?
SARA LEE. *(Doing all the motions.)* Cross my heart, hope to die, stick a needle in my eye.
BO BOB. Okay. I'm scered, Sara Lee. I'm scered to ask a woman out, 'cause I ain't never done it and I wudn't know what to do next. Yew know, the holdin' hands, kissin' and whatnot.
SARA LEE. My favorite part is the whatnot.

BO BOB. See there, yew don't take me serious.

SARA LEE. Oh no, honey—yew are wrong. Dead wrong. Let me show yew somethin'. (*SHE goes to the door. Looks out the window and locks the door.*)

BO BOB. What are yew doin'?

SARA LEE. Yew'll see. (*SHE dims the lights.*) Welcome to Sara Lee's School of Romance. I am Sara Lee Turnover, your instructor for today.

BO BOB. Yew are?

SARA LEE. I am. (*Approaching Bo Bob.*) Lesson number one is in the art of kissin'.

BO BOB. It is?

(*SHE throws her arms around him and kisses him madly HE, at first, is in shock, then goes for it with gusto. THEY finally take a break.*)

SARA LEE. Good-niss, Bo Bob. Yew better git on down to Bluebell's. Yure ready!

(*BO BOB excitedly grabs his hat and mail bag and hurries out the door. SARA LEE congratulates herself in the mirror and exits into the back room of the salon as the LIGHTS go down*)

ACT I

Scene 6

Lowake Inn, Bluebell's bar.
Full LIGHTS come up as ...

CHEATIN' 37

SID walks into Bluebell's, singing. HE cleans off the table, walks over to the bar to put the dirty dishes away. MAYBELLINE comes out of the bathroom, not wanting Sid to recognize her. SID sees her backside as SHE walks to the table. SHE sits away from him.

SID. May I help ya, miss?
MAYBELLINE. (*Disguises her voice.*) I'd like a martini on the rocks ... two olives, please.
SID. A martini, huh? Don't git many calls for them. (*Picks up a bar manual, blows dirt off it and looks through it.*) Mar ... mar ... martini. Let's see. Yeah, here it is. This 'un's gonna take some doin'.

(MAYBELLINE gets situated, HE makes the drink.)

SID. (*To audience.*) Must be one of them whores blowed in from Abilene.

(MAYBELLINE lights a cigarette, blows a couple of rings in the air.)

SID. Yew from out of town, miss?
MAYBELLINE. Could be. What's it to ya?
SID. Not a whole hell of a lot. (*To audience.*) Slut. (*HE gives her the drink.*)
MAYBELLINE. Thank yew. Sidney.
SID. Sidney? What the ...

(MAYBELLINE turns to him, full face.)

SID. Well, heavens-to-Betsy. Well, I'll be ... well,

lordy mercy ... well ...

MAYBELLINE. (*In her own voice.*) Well, whatdaya thank, cousin Sid?

SID. (*Walking away.*) I'm takin' the fifth.

MAYBELLINE. Well, be like that then. (*Concentrating on what she has learned.*) Let's see, a puff from the cigarette, then lift the martini to yure lips with the other hand, put yure little fanger out and ... (*SHE drinks and makes a face.*) Good Lord, this stuff tastes like horse piss. Sid, can I have a beer, please?

(*OVELLA rushes in out-of-breath, carrying the shotgun. SHE has run all the way from the motel to escape Teddy Joe's wrath*)

SID. Been duck huntin', Ovella?

OVELLA. (*Puts the gun down and approaches Maybelline.*) Excuse me, ma'am. Do yew thank yew could give me a lift home? Ya see, I'm havin' car trouble. I broke down up the street a bit, and I jest cain't seem to git it goin'. I jest live over on Elm Street.

MAYBELLINE. (*Disguises her voice.*) No. I'm, uh, sorry ma'am. But I walked here, and ...

OVELLA. Maybelline Cartwright, is that you?

MAYBELLINE. No, no ... it's somebody else. Yew must be mistaken.

OVELLA. (*Getting a better look*) Oh my gawd, it is yew! (*Laughing*) What the hell yew tryin' to prove, girl? (*Getting hysterical*) Was there a sale down at Woolworth on hairspray, bobby pins and cheap make-up?

MAYBELLINE. Fer yure information, Ovella Parsons...

OVELLA. Wilks.

MAYBELLINE. Wilks then. Fer yure information, Miz Wilks ... this is the doo, the very doo, that Cher wore to the Academy Awards two years ago.

OVELLA. Well, who gives a shit, Maybelline. Cher is a beautiful woman, thin as spaghetti, who can do jest about enythang with herself and git away with it. Put 'er in a toe sack and shave her bald and she'd still look good. (*Beat.*) Come to thank of it, the same effect might be an improvement fer yew.

MAYBELLINE. And who do yew thank yew are, Farah Fawcett?

OVELLA. We've been told we resemble.

MAYBELLINE. "We've been told?" I'm jest sure that someone's run up to Farah Fawcett sayin', "Do yew know yew look jest like Ovella Parsons? (*Hysterically laughing with SID.*) Sid, don't yew know that ol' Farah gits it all the time?

OVELLA. The name is Wilks ... yew stupid fat-ass retard.

SID. Whatch yure name-callin', Ovella. That's my cousin.

OVELLA. Yeah, well, that's yure problem.

MAYBELLINE. That's okay, Cousin Sid, but I can take care of myself. Retard? If yew'll remember Ovella, I was the one makin' all "A's" in Algebra II while some Farah Fawcett look-a-like was a flunkin' out of Basic Math number one with ol' lady Pritchard. Why even Bo Bob Jasper pulled a "B" in that 'un.

OVELLA. Well, maybe I was jest too busy to study with all my extracurricular activities. Somethin' yew wudn't know enythang about.

MAYBELLINE. The heck I wouldn't. The whole school knew about yure extracurricular activities. In fact, ever' football team in our district knew ya—Biblically!!

OVELLA. That's a flat-out lie and yew know it! Yew must have me confused with yure trampy girl friend, Sara Lee Turnover. I was always faithful to my then-to-be husband, Teddy Joe Wilks.

MAYBELLINE. Faithful? I didn't even know yew knew the meanin' of the word, Ovella. Come on, ever'body in Lowake knows yew been messin' around with Clarence Hopkins ever since day one in junior high school. Ever'body but poor ol' Teddy Joe. And from what I hear ... *it* has finally hit the fan.

OVELLA. What the hell are yew talkin' about?

MAYBELLINE. I jest come from Clara Bell's Dress Shop and she told me that Clement Barnes told her that Teddy Joe walked in on yew and Clarence in the Lowake Inn.

OVELLA. Well ... news travels fast.

MAYBELLINE. Oh my gawd, it's true! What happened? I want details!

OVELLA. Well, me and Clarence been meetin' at the Lowake Inn ever' Monday, and ...

MAYBELLINE. I already know that.

OVELLA. Yew do?

MAYBELLINE. Yeah, me an' the whole county.

SID. Cut the chit-chat and git on with the story.

OVELLA. Oh. Well, enyway, someone musta tipped Teddy Joe off 'cause he showed up mad as a hornet ... and I left him lookin' for Clarence in the motel room. And yew know what the Bible sez, Maybelline— "Seek and yew shall find." I have a feelin' Teddy Joe hath found.

(LIGHTS start to come up in the Lowake Inn and CLARENCE comes out of the bathroom, bloody, beaten up, with a black eye.)

OVELLA. I ran out 'cause I jest cain't stand the sight of blood. Now don't yew go and tell Sara Lee eny of this 'cause she'll have a canipshun fit and I don't want to have to deal with it. She already hates my guts enyway.

MAYBELLINE. *(Smiling.)* She shore does.

OVELLA. Yew wouldn't tell 'er ... wud ya now, Maybelline?

SID. *(To audience.)* Is a pig's ass pork?

OVELLA. Why yew ... *(Changing attitude for sarcasm effect.)* I'd give enythang to be like yew, Maybelline.

MAYBELLINE. Like me? Why?

OVELLA. 'Cause yure a fat-ass, and yew don't have to worry 'bout men, temptation and jealous husbands.

MAYBELLINE. *(Takes off after her)* That's it ...!!

SID. Yew can take her, Maybelline! I'd put money on it!

MAYBELLINE. I wudn't give one plug nickel to be enythang like yew, Ovella!

SID. *(To audience as HE exits to referee the fight.)* If she could catch 'er, she might jest kick 'er butt.

(The LIGHTS go down.)

ACT I

Scene 7

The Lowake Inn.
Full LIGHTS come up.
CLARENCE is doctoring himself, looking into the mirror.

TEDDY JOE. (*Offstage*) I'm really sorry I had to do that, Clarence, but yew had it comin'.

CLARENCE. Yeah, yeah. Shore I did.

TEDDY JOE. Can I git ya somethin'?

CLARENCE. Why don't yew grab us a couple of beers out of the sink there? You have a mean left hook, Teddy Joe.

TEDDY JOE. (*Entering with beers and a box of Band-Aids.*) Yeah, well, I learned that in the army. (*Hands Clarence a beer, opens his, then starts doctoring Clarence.*) Did you box in the navy, Clarence?

CLARENCE. What do yew thank?

TEDDY JOE. I found these here Band-Aids in the medicine cabinet in the can. They oughta help. I shore am sorry, Clarence, but yew had it comin'—messin' with Ovella and all.

CLARENCE. Okay, Teddy Joe, I had it comin'. I ain't gonna argue with ya.

TEDDY JOE. (*Putting on the Band-Aids*) There ain't any big-uns in here, Clarence. I'll jest have to make do with the little 'uns.

CLARENCE. Yew do that, Teddy Joe. I'm most appreciative.

TEDDY JOE. Yes sirree, Bob. I shore hated to do that

CHEATIN' 43

to yew 'cause I've always liked yew, Clarence.

CLARENCE. Yeah, well, I got that loud and clear.

TEDDY JOE. But yew had it comin', Clarence. Messin' with Ovella and all.

CLARENCE. Yure startin' to git on my nerves Teddy Joe—bad. Now if yew'll jest shut the hell up, I'd be most grateful.

TEDDY JOE. (*Finished with the Band-Aid job. It looks pretty silly.*) Well, that oughta do ya jest fine. (*Laughing as he makes his own joke.*) Jest take two aspirins and call me in the mornin'.

CLARENCE. Thank yew, Marcus Welby.

TEDDY JOE. Yes, sir, I've always liked yew, Clarence. Kinda wished we'd been better buddies all along.

CLARENCE. Well, maybe fate has finally smiled on us, Teddy Joe. I know it'd make my day. (*Pause.*) Listen, Teddy Joe. I giss I owe yew ... uh, I'm uh, I'm a real—well, shit. I jest wanna say—yew know.

TEDDY JOE. That yure sorry, Clarence?

CLARENCE. Yeah, yeah. That's it. That's it. Yew know, I never meant no harm. It's jest kinda got outta hand over the years—and I knew this was gonna happen sooner or later.

TEDDY JOE. (*Going after Clarence again.*) YEARS! Yew and Ovella been at this for years?!

CLARENCE. Now don't git yure dander up again, Teddy Joe!

TEDDY JOE. (*To himself*) Years ...

CLARENCE. Yew like bein' married, Teddy Joe?

TEDDY JOE. Yeah, I giss so. Most of the time it ain't so bad.

CLARENCE. I been thankin' about gittin' married myself lately.
TEDDY JOE. Yew and Ovella ain't thankin'...
CLARENCE. Hell no, she's married.

(TEDDY JOE gives him a look.)

CLARENCE. Yew know that. I don't know who. Sara Lee and me's been goin' together since the beginnin' of time, but ... yew know, it's kinda slim pickin's in Lowake. I been thankin' 'bout goin' over to Ballinger or Rowena—yew know, to check out the merchandise.
TEDDY JOE. It ain't like buyin' a car.
CLARENCE. I giss yure right. I do love Sara Lee, I really do—but ... yure gonna laugh at me, but lately ... I been thankin' about havin' kids. And, well ... it's kinda hard for me to thank of Sara Lee bein' a mama. Or me bein' a daddy for that matter. Yew know what I mean?
TEDDY JOE. Yeah, I do. I know what yew mean there, buddy. I don't thank Ovella would be no count at motherin' neither. I been wantin' kids for a few years now. I even hid her diaphragm onced.
CLARENCE. *(Starts to laugh.)* You hid her diaphragm?
TEDDY JOE. *(Also laughing.)* Yeah, but she jest held out till I gave it back. *(The TWO are hysterical.)* She's a selfish 'un. What'd yew see in her enyway?

(THEY exchange a look and immediately stop laughing.)

TEDDY JOE. Clarence, I thank yure wrong.
CLARENCE. 'Bout what?

CHEATIN' 45

TEDDY JOE. 'Bout Sara Lee. I thank that Sara Lee would make a damn good mama. She's about the best person I know.

CLARENCE. Aw, come on, Teddy Joe. Don't bullshit me. I don't like to be bullshitted.

TEDDY JOE. I ain't bullshittin' yew. I'm dead serious. And I thank yew'd make a damn good daddy, too. (*Joking, but serious.*) That is, if yew'd stop messin' around with other fella's wives.

CLARENCE. (*Pause.*) Yew know what? I thank yew may be right.

TEDDY JOE. (*Puts his arm around Clarence.*) I thank so, too. Let's go on over to Bluebell's. I'm buyin'.

(*LIGHTS start to come up in Bluebell's as:*
MAYBELLINE comes staggering in out of breath, followed by SID.)

CLARENCE. Okay.
TEDDY JOE. I sure am sorry that I had to do that to yew, Clarence, but you had it comin'.
CLARENCE. Jest shut the hell up, will yew?

(*The LIGHTS go down.*)

ACT I

Scene 8

Bluebell's Bar.
Full LIGHTS come up ... as MAYBELLINE sits at the table

talking to SID.

MAYBELLINE. I'm a failure, Cousin Sid, a pure-dee dyed-in-the-wool failure.
SID. Now don't be so hard on yureself, darlin'. Some day yure prince will come.

(BO BOB enters the bar, ready to sweep a woman off her feet.)

SID. Might not be today.
BO BOB. *(Noticing "the woman.")* Can I have my regular, Sid? Hello, miss.

(Avoiding eye contact with Bob Bob, MAYBELLINE waves "hello.")

BO BOB. Nice day.

(MAYBELLINE shakes her head "yes" still avoiding eye contact.)

BO BOB. Mind if I sit down?

(MAYBELLINE shakes her head "no." SHE picks up the martini glass and holds it in front of Bo Bob with her little finger out. BO BOB and MAYBELLINE face each other at the same time. BO BOB stifles a laugh as HE recognizes Maybelline.)

BO BOB. Maybelline Cartwright, is that yew?
MAYBELLINE. It's me, all right, Bo Bob. Sittin' here

as big as Dallas. Well, go ahead, Bo Bob—laugh—ever'body else has.

BO BOB. (*Trying to hold back his laughter.*) Well, naw Maybelline. I don't want to do that. I don't wanna laugh. I'm jest serprized, that's all. Yew know, I ain't never seen yew all gussied up like this before.

MAYBELLINE. (*A little emotional.*) Well, take a good hard look and lock it in yure mem'ry ... 'cause this is the first and the last time yure ever gonna see me like this.

BO BOB. And why's that, Maybelline?

MAYBELLINE. (*Starting to cry.*) 'Cause I'm fat and ugly and I look like a two-bit, two-ton whore.

SID. (*To audience.*) From Abilene.

BO BOB. (*Trying to comfort her.*) Now hush up, Maybelline. Hush up. Don't cry. That's jest not true.

MAYBELLINE. Yew sayin' I'm not fat?

BO BOB. Well, uh, well, no, Maybelline ... Yew are a large woman, but yew sure ain't ugly. Yew've got a right perty face. I've always thought that.

MAYBELLINE. (*Pulling back and looking right at him.*) Yew mean it?

BO BOB. Does ol' lady Barnes have varicose veins?

MAYBELLINE. (*Very happy.*) She shore 'nuff does. (*Hugs him. BO BOB doesn't know how to react.*) Oh, Bo Bob, that's the nicest thang enyone's ever sed to me. (*Kisses him on the cheek*) Yew are so sweet.

BO BOB. Well, good-niss, Maybelline. I don't know what to say.

MAYBELLINE. Don't say nuthin', Bo Bob. Yew've already sed enough.

(*SID has moved in to hear what they are saying.*)

BO BOB. Can I have a root beer, Sid?

(SID goes to get the root beer.)

MAYBELLINE. What do ya thank of my hair, Bo Bob? Do ya thank it's too gawdy?
BO BOB. Gawdy? Heck no ... it's ... it's a, well, it's kinda diff'rent, but I'm thankin' I like it.
MAYBELLINE. Yew do? What about my make-up?
BO BOB. It's fine, Maybelline, jest fine. But quite frankly, I don't thank a perty face like yures needs much make-up.
MAYBELLINE. *(Falling in love.)* Oh, Bo Bob, where'd yew learn to sweet talk a woman like that?
BO BOB. Aw, shoot, Maybelline, I don't know. I giss jest hangin' 'round Clarence ... maybe it jest rubbed off. Speakin' a Clarence, have yew heard what's happened?

(SID moves in to hear the dirt.)

MAYBELLINE. No, what? *(SHE moves closer to Bo Bob, too.)*
BO BOB. Well, I don't know if I should tell. I don't want to be spreadin' gossip.
MAYBELLINE. Tic-a-lock, tic-a-lock, Bo Bob. I'll carry it to my grave.
SID. *(To audience.)* She'll have to die in the next three minutes to keep that promise.
BO BOB. Well, due to some certain circumstances, that I cain't disclose, Teddy Joe Wilks has fine'ly found out about Clarence and Orvella.

MAYBELLINE. Oh, that. Yeah, we heard about it straight from the horse's mouth.

(SID has gone back to the bar.)

BO BOB. Whose?
MAYBELLINE. Ovella's.

(BO BOB laughs, then makes a horse sound. SID and MAYBELLINE also laugh.)

MAYBELLINE. She was in here jest a while ago. It seems that somebody tipped Teddy Joe off ... *(BO BOB reacts.)* ... and well, he jest walked in on her and Clarence down at the Lowake Inn and ... to tell the truth, I'm glad it happened, and I hope Sara Lee dumps Clarence for good this time.
BO BOB. Does she know?
MAYBELLINE. If she don't now, she will soon. I'll see to that.
BO BOB. Yew mean, yure gonna tell 'er?
MAYBELLINE. Durn tootin'. She's my best friend. It's best she hears it from me than third or fourth hand from one of them gossipy ol' hens down at her beauty shop.

(LIGHTS start to come up in the Out Coiffer. SARA LEE enters and talks out the door.)

SARA LEE. Don't worry about it, Clara Bell. Thanks fer tellin' me. I'll be all right. *(SHE closes the door and stands against it, thinking.)*

BO BOB. *(After awhile.)* Maybelline, yew don't thank that Sara Lee's been in the dark about this all these years, do yew?

MAYBELLINE. I thank that Sara Lee believes what she wants to believe, but this time, she's gotta believe the truth. She ain't gotta choice.

(SARA LEE exits to the back of the Oui Coiffer.)

BO BOB. I giss yure right. I shore do hate to see 'em split up. I always kinda liked 'em together.

MAYBELLINE. *(Impressed.)* Yew know, Bo Bob, yure a nice human bein'. Yew really are.

BO BOB. And yure a nice human bein' too, Maybelline.

MAYBELLINE. I am?

BO BOB. Yes, yew are. *(HE moves closer to her.)*

MAYBELLINE. Yew really thank so?

(THEY move closer still.)

BO BOB. I shore do.

(THEY kiss. Awkward at first, then MAYBELLINE goes for the gusto. SHE is definitely the dominant one here. THEY finally take a breather.)

BO BOB. Holy Cow!! Where did yew learn to do that, Maybelline?

MAYBELLINE. I used to practice on my stuffed animals, but they never kissed me back. Oh Bo Bob, yew made me feel like a woman for the first time in my life. It's kinda like when yew go to the dentist's office and git a shot of that tingly stuff. Oh, Lord in Heaven, help me control myself! (*SHE attacks him again, more passionate than ever.*)

BO BOB. Well, good-niss, Maybelline. I never ...

SID. (*To audience.*) It's the truth. He never.

BO BOB. Have yew ever taken a ride in a mail truck?

MAYBELLINE. (*Giggling.*) Uh, un. (*Shaking head "no."*)

BO BOB. Wud yew like to?

MAYBELLINE. (*Still giggling.*) Uh-huh.

(*Shaking head "yes" as HE takes her hand and THEY exit, giggling all the way.*)

SID. (*Following them.*) I ain't never seen inside one either, Bo Bob. Is it a GMC?

(*The LIGHTS go down.*)

ACT I

Scene 9

Oui Coiffer Salon.
Full LIGHTS comes up.
CLARENCE knocks on the Oui Coiffer door. SARA LEE comes out of the back room, crying.

SARA LEE. Who is it?

CLARENCE. (*Offstage.*) It's me, Sara Lee, Clarence.
SARA LEE. Clarence who?
CLARENCE. (*Offstage.*) Clarence Hopkins.
SARA LEE. Clarence Hopkins, huh? Well, yew go away. I have nothin' to say to yew—yew low down, scum-of-the-earth, rotten-to-the-core, two-timin', cheatin', sorry son-of-a-bitch!
CLARENCE. (*Offstage.*) Well, I'm glad yew didn't have nothin' to say. C'mon Sara Lee—let me in. I wanna talk to yew.
SARA LEE. Well, I don't want to talk to yew ... now or never. So git outta here and git outta my life forever.
CLARENCE. (*Offstage.*) C'mon Sara Lee. Jest give me five minutes. Jest five minutes, then I'll leave yew alone.
SARA LEE. I can hear yew jest fine from out there.
CLARENCE. (*Offstage.*) I ain't talkin' through no keyhole, Sara Lee.
SARA LEE. Five minutes, huh?
CLARENCE. (*Offstage.*) That's all. Then I'll leave. Jest five minutes.

(*SARA LEE opens the door; CLARENCE enters, SHE sets the timer.*)

SARA LEE. The clock is tickin'.
CLARENCE. I've made a mistake, Sara Lee. A very big mistake.
SARA LEE. (*Looks at the timer.*) Go ahead, yew've got a whole four minutes and fifty seconds left.
CLARENCE. Aw, c'mon Sara Lee. Let's jest talk. Let's jest clear the air.
SARA LEE. As far as I'm concerned, the air is clear.

(*Sniffs.*) See, I'm breathin' real deep. Yes sir, I'm startin' my life over. I've wasted ten years of my life on some sorry mechanic, waitin' fer nuthin'—but no more. No sirree. That's it. Yew've made yure bed. Now sleep in it with whoever yew by-gawd please.

CLARENCE. (*Approaches her.*) Sara Lee, I'm sorry. It's over, Sara Lee. All over between me and Ovella. It's jest me and yew now, baby. (*Touches her.*)

SARA LEE. (*Slaps his hand away with rat tail comb*) Don't yew touch me. Don't yew dare touch me after what yew've done. And don't call me baby.

CLARENCE. I sed I was sorry.

SARA LEE. Well, sorry jest don't cut it this time, buddy. (*Looks at timer.*) Yew've got exactly two minutes and forty-five seconds left.

CLARENCE. Sara Lee, I want yew to marry me.

SARA LEE. Yew what?

CLARENCE. (*Takes ring out of his pocket.*) I want yew to marry me, Sara Lee. I've had this ring for two years. I've jest been waitin', hopin', for the right time to give it to yew. I got it over at the jewelry department of Heidinheimer's. I want yew to marry me, Sara Lee.

SARA LEE. (*Looking at ring*) Yew know, Clarence. Yure even sorrier than I thought yew were. Jest who the hell do yew thank yew are doin' this to me?

CLARENCE. Doin' what, baby? I'm trying to straighten out somethin'.

SARA LEE. Yeah, well—I ain' no car fender.

CLARENCE. I need yew, Sara Lee. I need yew, baby.

SARA LEE. Quitcha callin' me baby. And yew sure as hell don't need me. What yew need, Clarence, is a woman. And eny woman will do. I'll do. Ovella will do. Maybe even ol' Maybelline will do. Although she's too good fer yew. It really doesn't matter who, does it, Clarence? Jest so long as yew git a little from time to time.

CLARENCE. That ain't true. It does too matter. It does, Sara Lee. I love yew, I do. Sure, I've been messin' with Ovella for a long time, and I was wrong. Dead wrong. Cain't yew see that, Sara Lee? I sed I was sorry. What else yew want me to do? Yew want me to git down on my knees and beg? Huh? Is that what yew want? Okay. (*HE does.*) I'm on my knees now, Sara Lee. I'm beggin' yew to forgive me. I'll be faithful to yew this time, baby. I will. I'm sorry. I'm so sorry.

SARA LEE. And so am I, Clarence. Y'know, I've waited a long time for this. For yew to ask me to marry yew. And now ... and now ... now I don't care. I don't give a royal shit. Yew lied to me, Clarence. For years yew lied. And I lied to myself. Yew thank I didn't know? Yew really thank ol' Sara Lee's that dumb?

CLARENCE. No I don't ...

SARA LEE. Hell, I knew all along. I jest didn't want to believe it. And ever' time I was fixin' Ovella's hair on her Monday afternoon standin' appointment ... gettin' ready fer yew, Clarence—I wanted to spill some chemical on her hair to make 'er go bald. That wudda got her goat. But I didn't. I didn't. And yew know why?

CLARENCE. No.

SARA LEE. Because I'm a professional. (*SHE looks at the timer.*) Yure five minutes is up, Clarence. Have a good life.

CLARENCE. (*Gets up, lingers a second.*) I love yew, Sara Lee. (*HE exits.*)

SARA LEE. Bye, bye, Clarence.

End of Act I

ACT II

Scene 1

Bluebell's Bar.
LIGHTS come up and...
SID enters from the back room, CLARENCE behind him,
  coming from the restroom.

SID. (*To audience.*) Shoo-wee! I wudn't trade places with eny of 'em for all the tea in China, I'm a tellin' ya—there wudn't talk 'bout enythang else in this town for days. Yew know, gossip, gossip, gossip. (*All very hush-hush.*) Now, Clarence sat there at that very table for at least five days. Aw, he went home ever' night long 'bout midnight—that's when I close. But he was here ever' mornin' bright and early when I opened. I shoulda charged him rent. Now Otis, Clarence's brother, he ain't in this story. He sed he wudn't gonna take much more of it. Sed that Clarence better git the bug outta his ass and git back to work. Let's see if I can cheer him up. You see, me and Clarence used to sing duets over at the first Baptist Church of Lowake on "Singsperation Night." That was before Lowake voted wet and before I bought Bluebell's. The Baptists don't much care for drankin' ... I'm a Methodist now. This here is Clarence's favorite hymn. (*Picks up his guitar, sits at the table, and starts to play and sing [music at back of script].*) "Oh, they tell me of a home far beyond the skies. Oh, they tell me of a home far away. Oh, they tell me of a home where no storm clouds rise. Oh, they tell me of an uncloudy day." Come on Clarence, chime on in. Yew know this is yure favorite hymn. 'Member them "Singsperations"?

CLARENCE. Shut up, Sid.

SID. (*To audience.*) See what I mean? (*Continues song.*) "Oh, they tell me that He smiles on His people there, and..."

CLARENCE. It's *children*.

SID. Children. "And His smile takes their sorrow all aw..."

CLARENCE. It's *drives*. "*Drives* their sorrow all away."

SID and CLARENCE. "And they tell me that no tears will ever come again, in that lovely land of uncloudyday..."

(*THEY finish the verse and chorus in harmony to a big finish.*)

SID. Now don't that make yew feel better?

CLARENCE. Shit, no!

SID. C'mon Clarence. Yew gotta shake this. Yew cain't go on mopin' around here forever.

CLARENCE. Sid, there ain't nothin' gonna drive my sorrows away. I am one whupped pup. Gimme another beer, will ya?

SID. Comin' right up, Clarence. (*As HE's getting the beer, to audience.*) See what I mean? Jest a mournin' over losin' ol' Sara Lee. Wudn't even take that engagement ring he bought 'er down at Heidinheimer's. I don't rightly blame 'er. Yew shoulda seen that thang.

CHEATIN' 57

(BO BOB walks into Bluebell's.)

BO BOB. Hey Clarence, hey Sid. Nice day, ain't it?
CLARENCE. Accordin' to who, Bo Bob?
BO BOB. Accordin' to me—Bo Bob Jasper. And that weatherman, Bill Johnson, on Channel Five sed so, too. *(HE sits and starts sorting his mail.)*
CLARENCE. And I giss that makes yew two the by-gawd-dispute-me-not-truth-authorities on what kinda day it is.
BO BOB. Well, naw, Clarence. I was jest sayin' ...
CLARENCE. And I'm jest sayin' that it ain't a nice day!
BO BOB. Okay, Clarence. If yew say so.
CLARENCE. Yew know what kind of day it is, though?
BO BOB. Naw, I cain't say as I do. That weatherman, Bill Johnson, on Channel Five sed ...
CLARENCE. Wud yew jest shut the hell up 'bout that sissyfied, plaster-haired, homasexual—Bill Johnson?!
BO BOB. I didn't know he was one of *them.*
SID. Hell, he makes Richard Simmons look like Clint Eastwood. Why that whole newscast is a nest of sissies.
CLARENCE. That's a fact. And another fact is that it ain't a nice day. In fact, it's the by-gawd, worst, shittiest, day of my life.
BO BOB. And why's that, Clarence?
CLARENCE. Don't play dumb with me, Bo Bob. Yew know why. A fella loses his girl friend and his mistress all in the same day and yew ask me a dumb-ass question like, "And why's that, Clarence."
BO BOB. Well, Miz Pritchard always told me that no

question was too dumb to ask.

SID. (*To audience.*) She give Bo Bob a "B."

CLARENCE. Well, thanks fer bringin' up that ol' bag on the worst day of my life.

BO BOB. Well, good-niss, Clarence. I thought that after five days yew'd be gittin' over it. I thought that the day it happened, that that would be "the by-gawd worst day of yure life," un-quote. (*HE knocks the mail off the table.*)

CLARENCE. Well, my-oh-my, yew've been doin' a whole lotta thinkin' there, haven't yew, Bo Bob? Who'da thought?

BO BOB. (*Picking up the mail.*) Clarence, what makes this *the* worst day, compared to the past five days?

CLARENCE. Thank yew fer askin' that questin, Bo Bob. (*Takes two tickets from his pocket.*) See these?

BO BOB. Yeah, what're they for?

CLARENCE. These here're two tickets to the George Jones concert performin' live in Abilene, Texas. Now who's my favorite sanger, Bo Bob?

BO BOB. Male or female?

CLARENCE. Male, asshole.

BO BOB. Yew don't have to get nasty about it. I giss it's a toss-up 'tween Merle Haggard and George Jones. Of course, you always liked, "Good Ol' Boys Like Me" by Don Williams, and then there was that Willie Nelson song yew played all summer long on yure Victrola player ...

CLARENCE. Could yew jest shut up for one-half second, Bo Bob. Cain't you jest listen?

BO BOB. Well, yew asked me who yure favorite sanger was, and I was jest makin' a list of all the sangers yew liked to listen to ...

CLARENCE. SHUT UP!! (*Silence*.) Thank yew. I am tryin' my damndest to explain why this is the by-gawd, worst shittiest day of my life!

BO BOB. And why's that, Clarence?

CLARENCE. (*Slowly, angry, but trying not to lose it.*) Because I'm sittin' here with a dumb-ass shit-head that talks too much and I've got these two tickets here to see George Jones live in concenrt in Abilene, Texas. And I ain't got nobody to go with. And it's Saturday.

BO BOB. Well, why didn't yew say somethin', Clarence. I'll go with yew.

CLARENCE. Yew will? Well, thank yew, Bo Bob. What a generous offer. What fun! What fun!

BO BOB. Aw, thank nothin' of it, Clarence. What are friends for?

CLARENCE. I don't know, Bo Bob. (*To Sid.*) What are friends for? They sure as hell ain't fer goin' to concerts with. That's what women are for, Bo Bob. Bit I giss yew wouldn't know nothin' 'bout that since yew hadn't had a date with one since Gawd created Adam and Eve. Ya know Sid, sometimes I thank Bo Bob is more homasexual than that Bill Johnson on Channel Five.

BO BOB. Yew take that back, Clarence. (*Jumps up attacking Clarence.*) I sed, take it back!

CLARENCE. Okay, okay. I take it back. That was joke, Bo Bob. Cain't yew take a little joke?

BO BOB. Yeah, but that wadn't funny. 'Sides, I had me a date with Maybelline Cartwright on Monday, and we're goin' out agin for supper tomorra night.

CLARENCE. Well, spit in the fire and call the dogs. Maybelline Cartwright, huh?

BO BOB. (*Proudly.*) Yeah, I shore did.

CLARENCE. Bo Bob, Maybelline Cartwright is the ugliest woman south a Dallas.

SID. I'd watch it Clarence. That's my cousin.

CLARENCE. I'm sorry, Sid, but I've seen butts that are better lookin' than Maybelline's face.

SID. (*To audience.*) Sometimes the truth hurts.

BO BOB. Whose ... b-b-bohind is better lookin'?

CLARENCE. Well, I ain't gonna get specific 'bout it.

BO BOB. Well, I giss she's by-gawd better lookin' than yure date tonight to that George Jones concert in Abilene.

CLARENCE. Aw, I don't know 'bout that, Bo Bob. I've always thought yew were pertier than ugly ol' Maybelline Cartwright. (*Getting up.*) C'mon, Bo Bob. Let's git over to Abilene early. We can go to the bowlin' alley and pick up some cheap women.

(*LIGHTS start to come up in the Out Coiffer and ..
OVELLA enters*)

OVELLA. Sara Lee!

BO BOB. I don't know 'bout that. No rain, no sleet, no George Jones concert is gonna keep me from deliverin' this mail.

CLARENCE. Well git the lead out, buddy. I'll help yew deliver that mail. (*As THEY exit Bluebell's.*) They say that Tammy Wynette may show up and ...

SID. (*Following them out, grabbing his bowling bag from behind the bar.*) If yew boys don't mind, I'd like to bowl a few frames myself.

(*The LIGHTS go down.*)

ACT II

Scene 2

Oui Coiffer Salon.
Full LIGHTS come up and ...
SARA LEE enters from the backroom and sees OVELLA.

OVELLA. Oh, good afternoon, Sara Lee. Do yew thank yew could do my hair right quick before yew close?

SARA LEE. I'm busy, Ovella. It's time fer my stories on TV. And what happened to appointments, Ovella? What do yew thank this is ... Super Cuts in San Angelo?

OVELLA. Oh, come on, Sara Lee. Yew know yure never that busy.

SARA LEE. For yure information, missy, Oui Coiffer is the only beauty shop in Lowake, which makes me a very busy professional hair dresser, thank yew very much.

OVELLA. I ain't gonna stand here and argue with yew, Sara Lee. I need a quick comb out because I'm goin' out tonight.

SARA LEE. Yew are, are yew? And what poor fella have yew managed to rope into takin' yew out this time? Yew've been through ever' eligible bachelor in Lowake since Teddy Joe left yew on Monday. And from what I hear, some of 'em wadn't that eligible. Otis Hopkins sed he even got lucky with yew, and he's got a wife and three younguns.

OVELLA. Well, quite frankly, that is none of yure business, Sara Lee. But jest to set the record straight,

Teddy Joe did not leave me. In fact, he begged me to stay—but I felt that a trial separation is necessary fer us to reevaluate our feelin's for one another.

SARA LEE. Seems like I heard Penny sayin' those exact words the other day on "Search For Another World."

OVELLA. Are yew gonna do my hair or not, Sara Lee?

SARA LEE. Not—Ovella!

SARA LEE and OVELLA. Bitch.

(OVELLA starts to walk out the door. SARA LEE spots the chemical that she's always wanted to put on Ovella's hair.)

SARA LEE. Well, what the heck, Ovella. I giss I have time fer one more comb out. Sit down.

OVELLA. Oh, thank yew, Sara Lee. I owe yew one for this.

(SHE sits down and SARA LEE starts on her hair.)

SARA LEE. Jest a tip this time would be nice, Ovella.

OVELLA. I thought yew weren't supposed to tip the owner of the shop.

SARA LEE. Well, I'll make an exception for yew.

OVELLA. Much obliged.

SARA LEE. So, where's the big date tonight, Ovella? And who is the luck ... the poor victim?

OVELLA. I'm goin' to the George Jones concert in Abilene with Ernest Wheelis.

SARA LEE. Yure goin' with my third cousin on my mama's side, Ernest Wheelis? Why yure old enough to be his ...

OVELLA. Don't yew dare say "mother."

SARA LEE. Does my Aunt Hatti know about this?

OVELLA. Well, I don't know, Sara Lee. Surely a nineteen-year-old bo ... man can make his own date decisions without runnin' to his mama for permission.

SARA LEE. I'll take that as "No, Hatti dudn't know a thang about it." She'll shit a gold brick when she finds out. And she will find out, Ovella.

OVELLA. Aw, fiddle-sticks, Sara Lee. It ain't that big-a-deal.

SARA LEE. Well, it will be to Ernest. He's been goin' with that cute little virgin Baptist girl, Sissy Jones. He'll be tickled pink to go out with a married woman who'll bed flop with enythang that moves.

OVELLA. I'm ignorin' yew, Sara Lee Turnover. (*Starts singing.*)

SARA LEE. Go ahead and ignore, Ovella. I'll jest chatter to myself. (*To self as OVELLA sings louder.*) Yew know, sugar, I thank that Ovella Parsons is the biggest slut in Concho County. (*In another voice; OVELLA sings louder.*) I agree, honey bunch. She broke up Clarence and Sara Lee, didn't give it a second thought. I heard she waltzed right in to Sara Lee's Oui Coiffer the very week and asked her to do her hair ... didn't even have an appointment. Why, her daddy would roll over in his grave. (*First voice again as OVELLA gets madder and louder.*) What a fine, Christian woman she was ... and to thank that she produced such a dyed-in-the-wool tramp!

OVELLA. (*Breaking.*) Cut it out, Sara Lee! Jest cut out the horseshit and fix my hair!

SARA LEE. I'm sorry, Ovella. I jest got carried away. I tell yew what. Jest to make it up to yew, I'm gonna give yew somethin' extra special. Somethin' I jest got in today. It's a treatment for damaged hair.

OVELLA. Well that's awful nice of yew, Sara Lee ... even though my hair ain't damaged like some people I know with a cow pile on their head.

SARA LEE. (*Patronizing.*) Yure so right, Ovella. (*SHE opens the treatment.*) I so do wish I had perty hair like yew. (*Pours it on.*) And after this treatment, ever'body will be commentin' on yure hair. That's guaranteed. (*Rubs it in.*)

OVELLA. (*Pause.*) That stuff kinda burns.

SARA LEE. (*Reading the directions*) Burns? Well, that's funny. It's not supposed to. I wonder what's wrong?

OVELLA. (*Suddenly panicking.*) Oh my gawd, Sara Lee! My gawd! It feels like my head's on fire! Rinse it out! Rinse it out! (*Runs around the room*) Oh my gawd! My head's on fire! Rinse it out ...!!

SARA LEE. (*Calmly.*) Un-oh, silly me. I fogot to dilute it. How could I have been so careless?

(OVELLA exits screaming. SARA LEE looks in her towel and pulls out a cluster of hair)

SARA LEE. Oops! (*SHE smiles.*)

(LIGHTS go down as...
SARA LEE exits to the back room of the Oui Coiffer, pleased)

ACT II

Scene 3

The Lowake Inn.
LIGHTS come up as ...
CLARENCE comes crawling out of the bathroom, drunk, in his boxer shorts. HE is singing a hymn at the top of his lungs There is a KNOCK at the door.

CLARENCE. Go away! (*HE continues singing and finds a whiskey bottle in the messy room. HE drinks and sings; the KNOCK continues*) Go away!

MAYBELLINE. (*Enters the room, scarf on her head, wearing a coat, sunglasses, not wanting to be recognized. SHE goes to Clarence*) Clarence?

CLARENCE. (*Turns around, she scares him to death*) AUGH!

MAYBELLINE. Clarence ...

CLARENCE. Maybelline, is that yew?

MAYBELLINE. It's me all right.

CLARENCE. What are yew doin' here?

MAYBELLINE. Bo Bob told me to come over here and talk some sense into yew. Otis told me to come over here and knock some sense into yew—and Sara Lee told me to come over here and kick the yew-know-what outta yew.

CLARENCE. Who's advice yew gonna take?

MAYBELLINE. I haven't decided yet. I'm gonna start with Bo Bob's and then proceed to Otis; and if that don't work, then I'll work on down to Sara Lee's. (*Shows her boots to him.*) See, I wore my boots.

CLARENCE. (*Looking at her attire.*) Is it already winter?

MAYBELLINE. (*Laughing*) Naw, naw ... (*SHE starts dressing him very motherly.*)

CLARENCE. Good, I thought I mighta missed a couple a seasons.

MAYBELLINE. I jest didn't want to be recognized comin' to a motel room known to be occupied by the biggest heathen in West Texas. Yew know the gossips in this town.

CLARENCE. Not like yew do, Maybelline. Where are my cigarettes?

MAYBELLINE. I don't know how you find enythang! (*Looking around, starts to clean up*) Oh, Clarence. What's become of yew? You've lost all yure pride. Yure stoopin' oh so low. Why, yure livin' like white trash. Pure-dee white trash. (*Points to bathroom.*) And this place smells like poor people.

CLARENCE. I feel like poor people. (*Seeing the Bible, HE reads silently.*) Oh, looky here, it's the Holy Bible—placed by the Gideons. (*HE reads a scripture*)

MAYBELLINE. Good. Maybe we're gittin' somewhere now. Sometimes yew have to be lookin' up from the bottom before yew can see the light at the end of the tunnel. Sometimes yew have to sink to the pits of hell...

CLARENCE. I don't wanna go to hell, Maybelline.

MAYBELLINE. Well, yew better straighten up and fly right. 'Cause yew got one foot in already and yure never gonna git that pot o' gold at the end of the rainbow. Sometimes yew have to start at the bottom rung before yew can climb Jacob's ladder. Sometimes ...

CLARENCE. Okay, Maybelline, I got it. Good Lord,

yure startin' to sound like Bo Bob Jasper.

MAYBELLINE. And what's wrong with that?

CLARENCE. Nothin' wrong with it at all if yew like soundin' like a dumb-ass shit-head.

MAYBELLINE. Don't yew ever git tired of puttin' people down, Clarence? Pokin' fun? Talkin' behind peoples back?

CLARENCE. I don't say nothin' 'bout nobody I wudn't say to their face.

MAYBELLINE. Oh really? Then why don't yew jest kiss my butt, Clarence? But remember (*Indicating*)—this is my butt and this is my face! Didn't want yew to git mixed up bein's I heard yew have trouble tellin' my face from some of the more prominent butts of Lowake.

CLARENCE. Maybelline, I didn't mean nothin' by that. It was jest a joke. Yew know, men talk. Cain't enybody take a joke?

MAYBELLINE. Jest listen at yew, Clarence. Yure whole life is one big joke. (*À la sergeant.*) Stand up, soldier! I said, stand up! (*SHE grabs him by the hair and lifts him to his feet.*) Now, take a look at yureself in the mirror! (*SHE yanks his head towards the mirror over the bed.*) I said ...

CLARENCE. Okay, I'm lookin'!

MAYBELLINE. What do yew see, soldier? I cain't hear yew! WHAT DO YEW SEE!!?

CLARENCE. (*Starts to cry softly.*) I see a loser.

MAYBELLINE. I CAIN'T HEAR YEW, SOLDIER! WHAT DO YEW SEE?!

CLARENCE. (*Yelling with tears, anger.*) I SAID, I SEE A LOSER! A real loser. (*In tears*) I'm a loser, Maybelline. I've lost ever'thang. I lost Sara Lee. Nobody loves me, Maybelline. Nobody!

MAYBELLINE. Yure wrong, Clarence.

CLARENCE. Yew sayin' I'm not a loser?

MAYBELLINE. Well, naw, Clarence. That's not what I'm sayin'. But yew do have a lotta good points. (*Looking at his butt.*) A lotta good points.

CLARENCE. Yew really thank so?

MAYBELLINE. I really thank so.

(*CLARENCE moves closer and kisses Maybelline very passionately. THEY fall on the bed. SHE fights him off and gets up.*)

MAYBELLINE. No wonder Ovella's been cheatin' on Teddy Joe. Ooh—that was unbelievable, pure-dee unbelievable!

CLARENCE. I wanna make love to yew, Maybelline. I wanna make long mad passionate, rompin' love to yew. I wanna show yew what womanhood is all about.

MAYBELLINE. Womanhood? I gotta thank about this 'un for a minute. Oh my Lord—womanhood! (*SHE starts backing into the Out Coiffer.*)

(*LIGHTS start to dim in the Lowake Inn.*)

CLARENCE. Maybelline. Maybelline!! Maybelline!! (*CLARENCE has completely disappeared in the bed. The last "Maybelline" sounds distant.*)

(*LIGHTS go down.*)

CHEATIN'

ACT II

Scene 4

Oui Coiffer Salon.
LIGHTS come up as ...
MAYBELLINE backs into the Oui Coiffer and seats herself in the beauty chair. The audience now realizes that she has been dreaming SHE yawns TEDDY JOE enters the Oui Coiffer saying, "Maybelline" on top of Clarence's last "Maybelline."

TEDDY JOE. Maybelline ... Maybelline ... wake up!

MAYBELLINE. (*Jarred awake.*) I'm awake, I'm awake. I jest had the weirdest dream 'bout me and Clarence. He was sayin' "Maybelline, womanhood ..."

TEDDY JOE. Where's Sara Lee?

MAYBELLINE. She went over to Lawyer Pitman's to check on her malpractice insurance in casin' that Ovella sues.

TEDDY JOE. Well, I need to talk to her, so I'll wait.

MAYBELLINE. What about?

TEDDY JOE. That is none of yure business, Maybelline Cartwright.

MAYBELLINE. Well, I AM her best friend. And if yew don't tell me, then I'll jest hear it after'n yew leave.

TEDDY JOE. Well, if she so chooses to tell yew, that's fine—but I do not choose to do so.

MAYBELLINE. Yure gonna ask her out, ain't ya?

TEDDY JOE. My lips are sealed, Maybelline.

MAYBELLINE. Well, it makes sense. Ovella and Clarence are messin' 'round. Yew on the rebound, hit on

Sara Lee naturally jest to git even. Yes sirree, it makes sense to me. It shore does make sense.

TEDDY JOE. Yew are somethin' else, Maybelline.

MAYBELLINE. Well, am I right?

TEDDY JOE. (*Laughs.*) Well, it makes sense to me.

MAYBELLINE. I knew it, I knew it! Well, I don't thank so, Teddy Joe. I jest don't thank it's a good idea.

TEDDY JOE. Well, since I didn't ask for yure opinion, I don't give a rat's ass what yew think. (*Beat.*) Why not? Why don't yew thank it's a good idea?

MAYBELLINE. 'Cause it's comin' from an impure source.

TEDDY JOE. Well, what the hell's that supposed to mean?

MAYBELLINE. It means that yew ain't askin' her out 'cause yure interested in her. Yure askin' her out 'cause yure interested in gittin' back at Ovella and Clarence.

TEDDY JOE. Oh yeah? And how do yew know that I'm not interested in Sara Lee?

MAYBELLINE. Teddy Joe, how many times have yew asked Sara Lee out before this crap happened?

TEDDY JOE. Let's see ... twice't, I thank.

MAYBELLINE. Well, actually, yew asked her out three times and she went out with yew twice't.

TEDDY JOE. Holy Moses, Maybelline. Yure a by-gawd encyclopedia on other people's datin' activity.

MAYBELLINE. I keep up. Mine is so borin', I have to keep up with other people to stay awake. Enyway, yew asked her out three times and went out with her twice't. Once to the homecomin' dance and the other to that hayride the Lions Club had for them blind kids. Now why did yew ask her out those two times?

TEDDY JOE. 'Cause me and Ovella broke up for a spell.

MAYBELLINE. And as soon as Ovella come runnin' back, it was "forget ol' Sara Lee time."

TEDDY JOE. Well, naw, it was, well ... well she didn't care. She always had Clarence. It jest so happened that she was broken up with him those two times.

MAYBELLINE. And the time she turned yew down, she wadn't. I rest my case.

TEDDY JOE. And what case it that, Maybelline? Yew've got me all messed up. Drive it on home, Maybelline.

MAYBELLINE. Sara Lee never was interestin' enough to yew out and out. She was always a second choice, an afterthought. And yew were the same to her. So I thank if yew two go out right now, yure gonna git burnt. Yew play with fire, yew git burnt.

TEDDY JOE. Well, thank yew Dear Abby, for all that wonderful advice.

MAYBELLINE. You gonna take it?

TEDDY JOE. Hell no!

MAYBELLINE. Fine, jest be like that. But don't expect me to stay zipper-lipped when it don't work out, 'cause I'm gonna be the first to say "I told yew so."

TEDDY JOE. Fine. That's jest fine. (*Pause.*) I wonder what's takin' Sara Lee so long!

MAYBELLINE. Probably divine intervention. (*Pause.*) Teddy Joe, was yew ever in love with Ovella?

TEDDY JOE. Of course I was in love with Ovella. We was married for seven long years.

MAYBELLINE. That don't mean a thang. Lotsa people stay married fer years and they never love each other. Look at the Barnes.

TEDDY JOE. Well, in this case, there was love. At least from my end.

MAYBELLINE. What's it like?

TEDDY JOE. (*Thinking, distant.*) Well, when it's good, it's jest flat out wonderful. Jest the best feelin' that God allowed us human bein's to feel.

(*LIGHTS start to come up in Bluebell's as ...*
OVELLA enters, scarf on head, bald, drunk—a complete mess. SHE is singing very off key.)

OVELLA. (*Singing; ad-libbing melody.*) "I'm leavin' yew once agin."

TEDDY JOE. It's kinda like runnin' in a mountain clearin' with flowers all around, and God's beauty jest too much to behold.

OVELLA. (*Singing*) "And don't expect me to be yure friend."

TEDDY JOE. It's like wadin' in a stream, or sleepin' on the edge of that stream—and always with someone that means more to yew than yew mean to yureself.

OVELLA. (*Singing.*) "The way yew treated me, well it's a sin."

TEDDY JOE. And well, it's ... shoot Maybelline. Yew got me mush talkin'.

OVELLA. (*Singing*) "Forgive me, but I'm leavin' yew agin."

MAYBELLINE. Naw, Teddy Joe. That was beautiful. Pure-dee beautiful.

TEDDY JOE. Well, I'm gonna go find Sara Lee. (*HE exits.*)

MAYBELLINE. (*Calls out as SHE exits.*) No, don't do it! Take my advice. It's comin' from an impure source.

(*LIGHTS go down.*)

ACT II

Scene 5

Bluebell's
Full LIGHTS come up as
SID enters the bar OVELLA is behind the bar, looking for a drink, still singing.

SID. Yew should have seen 'em, Maybelline ... (*Spots Ovella.*) Ovella, what are yew doin' here? I left Maybelline in charge.
OVELLA. Yeah, well, I'd fire her ass if I was yew.
SID. I cain't. It'd break my Aunt Liddy Bell's heart. Yew shoulda seen her over at the Daughters of the Lone Star meetin'. Her favorite nephew, Sid Cranford, sangin' the "Star Spangled Banner." (*Picks up his guitar.*) Now I know how Elvis musta felt.
OVELLA. Dream on, Sid. (*Pointing to guitar.*) Can yew play that thang?
SID. Can Dolly Parton float?
OVELLA. Well, crank it up, cowboy. I wrote me a new song fer my show here tonight. Yew ain't the only one with talent in this town, ya know. I want yew to accompanapane ... accapelapane ... play along.

SID. What key?
OVELLA. What?
SID. What key?
OVELLA. J.
SID. (*Going along.*) J?
OVELLA. It's called, "I'm Leavin' Yew Agin." Yew ready?
SID. Yeah. (*HE strums a chord.*)
OVELLA. (*Singing.*)
I'm leavin' yew once agin,
And don't expect me to be yure friend,
The way yew treated me, well it's ...

(*OVELLA stops, not happy with Sid's performance.*)

OVELLA. Sid, could yew jest stay with me. Try to keep up. Let's take it agin from the top. Yew ready?

(*SHE starts up again, making up the song as she goes along. BO BOB enters, hears the music, starts clapping along, ready for a hoe-down.*)

OVELLA. (*Singing.*)
I'm leavin' yew once agin,
And don't expect me to be yure friend,
The way yew treated me, well it's a sin
Forgive me, but I'm leavin' yew agin.
BO BOB. (*Approaches Ovella and Sid.*) Howdy, Orvella. Hey, Sid. Nice day, ain't it? Can I have a root beer, Sid? (*SID complies; to Ovella.*) Yew mind if I sit down?
OVELLA. I don't give a shit.

BO BOB. That was real good, Orvella. Yew've got a real nice sangin' voice.

OVELLA. (*Stands up, picks up beer bottle and uses it for a mike.*) Well, thank yew, cowboy. And welcome to the Ovella Parsons show. Glad yew could make it. Now yew jest sit right there cowboy and take a load off. (*Interviewing with the beer bottle.*) I giss yew heard I was performin' here and rushed on down to catch my show. Hope yew didn't have too much trouble gettin' tickets.

BO BOB. Well, uh, no ... What the heck are yew talkin' 'bout, Orvella?

OVELLA. I'm talkin' 'bout me, cowboy. The biggest country and western queen in the U.S. of A. Bigger than Dolly. Bigger than Loretta. Even bigger than that mealy-mouthed Barbara Mandrell. I'm talkin' the biggest in the world. Julio Iglesias, eat yure heart out, wherever yew are! Me. Ovella Parsons.

BO BOB. Yure drunk, Orvella. And remember, yure name is Wilks—Orvella Wilks. Lord knows yuve reminded us all enuf times.

OVELLA. Well, I've changed it back—for professional reasons. And now I'm gonna sing fer yew my latest single, "Sometimes I Git Lonely." Hit it Sid!

(*SID plays and OVELLA begins to sing uptempo; ad-libbing melody*)

Yew walked out the door,
And didn't say goodbye,
Yew left without a warnin'
Yew didn't tell me why.

I thought I could make it,
Alone and on my own,
But babe, I jest cain't take it,
    There's one thang not known,

(It appears she has ended the song. SID puts his guitar down, then SHE starts up, slowing the song to a sad ballad SID grabs the guitar and plays along, BO BOB getting very sad as the song goes on)

OVELLA.
Sometimes I git lonely,
And sometimes I git sad
And sometimes I git lost
Among the feelin's we once had.

And sometimes, all night long
I cry myself awake.
Sometimes the lonely
    Is more than I can take.

(SHE is finished, and starts crying, falls in Bo Bob's lap and throws her arms around him)

    OVELLA. I'm so lonely, Bo Bob. I'm sooo lonely.
    BO BOB. (*Awkwardly.*) Gee whiz—aw, Orvella, now hush up.

(SHE continues to cry)

    BO BOB. Hush up, Orvella. Please. Good-niss.
    OVELLA. Nobody loves me, Bo Bob. Nobody.

Clarence, Teddy Joe. I lost 'em, Bo Bob. And now I'm bald, and I'll never git another damn date as long as I live.

BO BOB. Now, come on, Orvella. I heard 'bout that mishap over at Sara Lee's. It'll grow back.

OVELLA. It will not! I look like Reverend Tuttle—bald as a billiard ball. A man would have to be plum retarded to go out ... (*Realizing.*) Bo Bob, has enyone ever' told yew what a virile man yew are? A strong man, a real man, a he-man, superman—if yew know what I mean?

BO BOB. Aw. Orvella. Now, stop it. Yure drunk.

OVELLA. Well, I could sober up real fast.

BO BOB. Yeah, well, uh, I suppose yew could. (*Beat.*) Virile, huh?

OVELLA. (*Grabs Bo Bob and plants a long passionate kiss on him. HE is in shock.*) Let's yew and me go git a motel room over at the Lowake Inn, and I promise to teach yew things yew never knew existed.

BO BOB. Now, Orvella! (*Trying to get away.*) Stop it! Yew ain't yureself, and I'm gittin' all mixed-up up here. (*Points to his head.*)

OVELLA. Bo Bob, yew've always been all mixed-up up there. This don't take no Einstein.

BO BOB. That wasn't very nice, Orvella. I know I ain't no genius, but ...

OVELLA. Jest fergit it, dumb-dumb. I'm sure I can find someone else in this shit-hole to fulfill my needs. A woman does have needs, yew know.

(*SID starts singing, hinting he's available.*)

BO BOB. Orvella, please don't ever call me dumb-dumb agin. I don't much care for it.

OVELLA. Well, that's what yew are, dumb-dumb.
BO BOB. Stop it ...
OVELLA. Dumb-dumb, dumb-dumb, dumb-dumb ...
BO BOB. (*Losing it.*) Stop it, Orvella! Shut up! Jest shut the hell up! No wonder yew got so many problems. Yew're the nastiest bitch I've ever met. (*Catches himself.*) I'm sorry, Orvella. I didn't mean to call you that. I'm sorry.
OVELLA. Well, well, well, well, well. Mr. Goody-Two-Shoes has let down his Christian armor. Well, go on, Bo Bob. Tell me more. I wanta hear what yew and the rest of the town thanks of ol' Ovella Parsons. (*With beer bottle, interviewing.*) And sir, what do yew think of the talk of the town, Ovella Parsons?
BO BOB. Now, Orvella. I cain't do that. I don't want to do that.
OVELLA. We are on the air, Bo Bob, and yure makın' a complete fool outta yureself! (*Beat.*) Tell 'em—dumb-dumb!
BO BOB. Okay, I wıll! (*Grabs her beer bottle and talks into it.*) Nobody likes yew, Orvella. 'Cause yure rude, nasty, yew dump on people, yure self-centered, and yure jest down-right snooty.
OVELLA. Snooty?
BO BOB. And mean.
OVELLA. Snooty and mean, huh? (*Takes beer bottle back and turns to audience.*) Well, yew heard it yureselves, folks. This scoundrel, Ovella Parsons, is snooty and mean—and yew heard it straight from the mouth of this dumb-ass maılman! (*Long pause, then starts crying, sits.*) I don't wanta be mean, Bo Bob. I don't wanta be snooty. I wanta be nice. I wanta change. (*Crying out.*) I want Teddy

Joe. (*Puts head on table.*)

(*SID and BO BOB comfort her; SHE comes back up.*)

OVELLA. Or Clarence.

(*THEY walk away in disgust.*)

BO BOB. (*Returns.*) Orvella, Teddy Joe is a good man and don't yew forgit it.

(*HE exits out the front door. SID exits to the stock room. LIGHTS start to come up in the Lowake Inn and ... TEDDY JOE and SARA LEE enter the Lowake Inn, laughing.*)

OVELLA. (*Following Sid.*) Sid ... Sid ... Sid ... (*SHE exits.*)

(*LIGHTS go down.*)

ACT II

Scene 6

The Lowake Inn.
Full LIGHTS come up as ..
SARA LEE and TEDDY JOE look around the motel room after their big date

SARA LEE. Well, here we are at the Lowake Inn.

TEDDY JOE. Yeah, here we are ... jest the two of us.
SARA LEE. Who'd a thought. Not me ... that's fer sure.

(SARA LEE laughs nervously. TEDDY JOE has removed his shirt.)

SARA LEE. Teddy Joe, do yew mind if we jest talk fer a spell afore we start the ...
TEDDY JOE. The what?
SARA LEE. *(Laughs nervously.)* Yew know.
TEDDY JOE. Yeah, I know, I was jest crackin' a joke.
SARA LEE. Aw, yew was? *(Laughs now)* I git it now. *(Laughs.)* "The what?" Oh, that's funny. Ooooh weee, my sides ... my sides are achin'.
TEDDY JOE. So, what do yew want to talk about?
SARA LEE. *(Taking notice of Teddy Joe's shirtless body.)* Ya know, yew have a real nice body, Teddy Joe.
TEDDY JOE. Yeah, I know. I work out. Wanna feel my muscles? *(HE flexes for her.)*
SARA LEE. Oooo, them's are nice.
TEDDY JOE. *(Moves to her.)* Go 'head, feel 'em.
SARA LEE. *(SHE does.)* Oh my gawd! Them's are rock hard! Yew know, I don't believe I've ever seen muscles like that before up close. Clarence has muscles, but not like that. *(Feels again)* Much less felt 'em. Damn, them's are nice. I have seen 'em in them magazines, but hell, them guys look like freaks. That Arnold Schwartamajigger gives me the heebie-jeebies jest to look at 'im. Can yew imagine goin' to bed with 'im. Why he'd jest squash yure innerds right out.
TEDDY JOE. Yeah, well, them guys take steroids. I've

never took a steroid in my life. Mine's all natural. My philosophy is lean and mean, if ya know what I mean. (*HE has made another joke and laughs.*)

SARA LEE. (*Stalling.*) Teddy Joe, what are steroids?

TEDDY JOE. Well, they're a medication that are synthetic forms of testosterone and other male hormones. They are supposed to reverse the negative nitrogen balance and increase the use of protein to form additional muscle to those who work out and eat good.

SARA LEE. Well, Lordy mercy, Teddy Joe. That jest rolled right off yure tongue. Yew sound like a regular ol' licensed physician. Damn, that's really somethin'. Where'd yew learn that stuff?

TEDDY JOE. I read it in a muscle magazine. It was in a article called, "Steroids, Are They Fer Yew?" That's when I decided they wadn't fer me.

SARA LEE. Well, I declare. Yew know I read a lot, too. I have to subscribe to a whole slew of magazines bein's I run a beauty shop, yew know, fer the customers. (*SARA LEE takes Teddy Joe's coat and hangs it in the bathroom, offstage, and continues talking with the door closed.*) I read Cosmo like it was the Holy Bible. They have some real interestin' articles in there.

(*TEDDY JOE is undressing down to his shorts.*)

SARA LEE. Some people say it's jest flat out trash, but that ain't true. Clarence used to read it, too. Said Cosmo was jest as good as *Playboy* because of all them perty women in skimpy ...

(*SHE opens the door and TEDDY JOE is standing right in*

front of her in his briefs, SHE closes the door without missing a beat.)

SARA LEE. ... outfits. I thank when they's got some clothes on it's sexier, 'cause yew have to leave somethin' to the imagination. Those girls spread eagle in *Playboy* and *Penthouse* are plum disgustin'.

(TEDDY JOE opens the door and pulls SARA LEE out, gently.)

TEDDY JOE. Sara Lee, yew know what I thank?
SARA LEE. What?
TEDDY JOE. I thank yure stallin' on me.
SARA LEE. Yew know what I thank, Teddy Joe?
TEDDY JOE. What?
SARA LEE. I thank yure right.
TEDDY JOE. Are you scered?
SARA LEE. Yeah, a little, I giss.
TEDDY JOE. Yew scered of me?
SARA LEE. (*After a second.*) No.
TEDDY JOE. Then what is it, Sara Lee?
SARA LEE. I'm scered of ... I'm scered of ... I don't know how to put this, Teddy Joe. I giss I'm scered of the why's that we're doin' this.

TEDDY JOE. Yew been listenin' too much to Maybelline Cartwright.

SARA LEE. Maybe so, but ol' Maybelline has a good head on her shoulders. Enyway, I been thinkin' that the only real reason we're here is to git even, and I been thinkin' that that "why" jest ain't good enuf fer me.

TEDDY JOE. (*As HE is hugging her*) Well, it sure as

hell is good enuf fer me. And I hope they both find out about it.

SARA LEE. (*Takes his arms off her.*) That's what I mean, Teddy Joe. Yew would take me to bed right here in the Lowake Inn, in front o' God and the whole town and it wouldn't mean nothin' to yew, would it?

TEDDY JOE. But Sara Lee ...

SARA LEE. Jest hold yure taters. I ain't done! Yew would join yure body with mine and we'd become one in the eyes of God, jest like it says in the Bible. It's in one o' them Thessalonians I thank, and go on like it was nothin'. Yew would do that, Teddy Joe Wilks? (*Silence.*) Well, would ya?

TEDDY JOE. Well, I don't ...

SARA LEE. I ain't done, Teddy Joe! (*Pause.*) Do yew love Ovella, Teddy Joe?

TEDDY JOE. At this very moment, no I don't.

SARA LEE. I still love Clarence, Teddy Joe.

TEDDY JOE. Oh yew do, do yew? Well, I can certainly understand that, since he's been so good to yew.

SARA LEE. It hadn't all been bad.

TEDDY JOE. (*Picks up his pants and starts to put them on.*) Well, I giss that's a "no."

SARA LEE. I didn't exactly say that.

TEDDY JOE. (*Takes his pants off and goes after Sara Lee.*) Then I giss it means "yes."

SARA LEE. (*SHE escapes him. Panicking.*) I didn't say that neither.

TEDDY JOE. Then it's a "let's frustrate Teddy Joe" type o' decision. (*HE puts on his pants.*)

SARA LEE. Well, I'm sorry, Teddy Joe. I don't know what to do. I'm jest all mixed up. My mind's like Jello.

TEDDY JOE. (*Serious.*) What flavor? (*HE laughs at his new joke.*)

SARA LEE. Oh. Another joke?

TEDDY JOE. Right off the top. (*Pause.*) I'm gonna kiss yew, Sara Lee. We're gonna kiss for a long time. And at the end of that kiss yew either go on home ... or stick around here with me. It's gonna be yure decision.

SARA LEE. I don't know, Teddy Joe.

TEDDY JOE. Well, I do.

(*HE kisses her for a long time and THEY fall down on the bed and disappear.*
LIGHTS start to come up in Bluebell's as ...
SID enters the front door. HE looks over the headboard at Sara Lee and Teddy Joe and shakes his head.
LIGHTS go down in the Lowake Inn)

ACT II

Scene 7

Bluebell's
Full LIGHTS come up as ...
SID addresses the audience.

SID. Ain't this the biggest mess yew've ever seen in yure life? (*Pause.*) And quite frankly, that's the end of my story. Ya see, I don't have a endin' 'cause there ain't one yet. But ya'll want one, don't ya? (*Puts his hand on his head in the psychic position*) Oh, my Lord! It's a comin'!

(*Out of the psychic position and to audience.*) Ya'll do want a happy endin', don't ya? All right. I'll see what I can do. (*Back in the psychic position*) It's comin' on strong. I can feel it. Yes sir, I can see it now!! I see ...

(*BO BOB rushes in dressed in a fancy cowboy outfit.*)

BO BOB. Hey Sid. Nice evenin', ain't it?
SID. (*Does double take.*) Why I see Bo Bob Jasper.
BO BOB. Have yew seen Maybelline?
SID. She's in back takin' inventory. (*Calling*) Maybelline—yure Prince Charmin' is here.

(*A loud CRASH is heard offstage from the stock room*)

MAYBELLINE. (*Enering from stock room, totally in love*) Hey, Bo Bob. I was in back takin' inventory.
BO BOB. Nice evenin', ain't it, Maybelline?
MAYBELLINE. It shore is.
BO BOB. Maybelline. I kinda come over here to ask yew a question. (*Clears throat.*) I was wonderin' if yew would ...
MAYBELLINE. Yeah?
BO BOB. Well, I was wonderin' if yew wanted to ...
MAYBELLINE. To what, Bo Bob. What?
BO BOB. Could I have a root beer, Sid?
MAYBELLINE. I'll git it. (*MAYBELLINE brings the root beer.*)
BO BOB. Sit down, Maybelline. I was wonderin' ... I was wonderin' ...Well, I been thankin' 'bout them other ones ... Clarence, Sara Lee, Orvella, Teddy Joe. And I was thankin' that we're different, Maybelline. Diff'ent 'cause

... well, 'cause we got our feet on the ground, and we ain't livin' in some soap opery and ... I'd never do nuthin' to hurt yew. I love yew, Maybelline. (*HE kneels and takes out a ring and puts it on her finger*) And I'm wantin' yew to marry me. I bought this ring over at Abilene. No Heidinheimer's jew'ry department for my sweet Maybelline.

MAYBELLINE. (*Starts to cry.*) I love yew, too, Bo Bob. I cain't believe it.

(*Crosses to Sid and hugs him. SID is also crying.*)

MAYBELLINE. I ain't gonna be an old maid after all!

(*SHE and BO BOB begin to exit*)

MAYBELLINE. Now, the bridesmaids' dresses will be pink and white and they'll carry carnations, and Sara Lee will be the maid of honor, of course. And Clarence will be ...

(*THEY trail off; SID is all choked up*)

SID. (*Wiping his eyes. To audience.*) Ain't that somethin'. A grown man gittin' all teary eyed. Well, she is my cousin, ya know. Mr. and Mrs. Bo Bob Jasper. Kinda has a nice ring to it, don't it? Aunt Liddy Bell will be jest tickled pink. Finally gittin' to see her little girl, well, her girl, that is, walk down that aisle. (*Pause as HE cleans up a little.*) Yure not satisfied, are ya? Yure wonderin' about the other 'uns. Damn it, out-a-staters sure are hard ta please. (*Holds his head; he's getting something.*) Wait a minute. I jest felt somethin'. I'm gittin' it. It's Ovella...

CHEATIN' 87

(LIGHTS come up in the Lowake Inn as...
OVELLA enters, carrying her luggage, wearing
   conservative clothes and a nice wig)

SID. And she's transformed herself into a real live human bein'. Can that be right? *(SID goes aside and watches the scene from Bluebell's)*

(The Lowake Inn
OVELLA is unpacking a suitcase, and TEDDY JOE walks
   in from the bathroom, dressing.)

TEDDY JOE. Ovella?!
OVELLA. *(Startled.)* Teddy Joe?
BOTH. What are yew doin' here...?

(THEY laugh.)

OVELLA. Yew first.
TEDDY JOE. I had me a date. Thangs didn't work out.
OVELLA. I thought I'd stay here at the Lowake Inn jest to sort out my life. Yew know. They musta double booked the room. Sorry.
TEDDY JOE. Probably divine intervention, Ovella.
OVELLA. Ya think?
TEDDY JOE. Could be, Ovella.
OVELLA. Teddy Joe—Dave and Penny got back together today on "Search For Another World." Penny realized how wrong she had been and found that a trial separation wadn't the answer. *(Starts crying.)* I'm so sorry, Teddy Joe. I've been so awful. How will yew ever forgive

me?

TEDDY JOE. (*Consoling her, hugging.*) It's okay. I forgive yew. I love yew, Ovella.

OVELLA. I love yew too ...

(*SID blows his nose, loudly—he's touched.*)

TEDDY JOE. Let's go home now.

(*THEY start to exit OVELLA turns back.*)

OVELLA. (*Bitchy.*) Grab that suitcase!

(*HE does, THEY exit. LIGHTS go down. Bluebell's.*)

SID. (*To audience.*) I'm sorry. This is jest too much for me. A grown man, I swear. (*Pause, looks at audience.*) Now don't look at me that way. A fella can jest do so much. Two outta three ain't bad. Ain't bad a tall. (*Giving in.*) Okay, I'll do what I can. But I ain't makin' no promises. (*HE exits into the stock room and continues talking.*) Why looky what I found. (*HE returns with red carnations.*) Carnations. Sara Lee's favorites. Now we'll jest put these over in the Oui Coiffer. Sara Lee should be back here eny minute. (*HE places them in the chair of the beauty shop.*) She always comes to the Oui Coiffer to thank thangs out. And I have a feelin' she's gotta lot to thank about after what almost happened with Teddy Joe tonight. (*HE returns to Bluebell's*)

(*The Oui Coiffer

CHEATIN' 89

LIGHTS come up in the Oui Coiffer as.
SARA LEE enters the beauty shop and spots the flowers.)

SARA LEE. Oh, Clarence. (*SHE picks them up.*)
CLARENCE. (*Enters the shop.*) Sara Lee.
SARA LEE. Oh, Clarence. They're beautiful.
CLARENCE. (*These are new to him, too.*) They are right perty, ain't they?
SARA LEE. I love yew.
CLARENCE. I love yew too, baby.
SARA LEE. Yew still have that ring from Heidinheimer's?
CLARENCE. Why no! I took it back. Yew said yew didn't want it ...
SARA LEE. Yew what?
CLARENCE. (*Takes the ring out of his pocket.*) I was jest kiddin'. It's right here. (*THEY kiss ; as THEY exit into Sara Lee's store room*) Let's hit that linoleum!

(LIGHTS go down.
Bluebell's.)

SID. Now wadn't that a piece a cake? Yew satisfied now? I know I am. Happy endin's. I love 'em. Shoo wee. All a that psychic activity's got me all tuckered out. (*Getting another vibe.*) Wait a minute. Another one's comin' on. It's a prediction. I predict that ever'thang's gonna be A-Okay from now on. No more cheatin', no more immorality—jest good clean livin'. Well, it's closin' time. It's been a long day. Ya'll drive careful goin' home. And watch out for eny armadillas crossin' the road. Don't wanta kill eny of our little Texas critters. Goodnight, all.

And ya'll come back to Bluebell's enytime yure in the neighborhood. Goodnight and may God bless.

BLACKOUT

The End

COSTUME PLOT

ACT I

Scene 1
SID
Wrangler jeans
Western shirt
Cowboy hat
Western belt

BO BOB
Mailman uniform
T-shirt
Black shoes

CLARENCE
Mechanic coveralls
White undershirt (tank)
Ugly green and gold boxer shorts
Lace-up work boots
Baseball cap

SARA LEE
Lee jeans
Western shirt
Cowboy boots
Long earrings
Timex wristwatch

OVELLA
Fringe western shirt

Gray miniskirt
White cowboy boots
Long earrings
Hot pink scarf

TEDDY JOE
Running shorts
Tank top
Tennis shoes
White athletic socks

MAYBELLINE
White waitress uniform
Royal blue apron
White nurses shoes
Stockings

Scene 2
OVELLA
Purple corset
Purple stockings
Purple garter
Clothes from Scene 1 scattered around room

CLARENCE
Boxers (that were under overalls)
Clothes from Scene 1 scattered around room

Scene 3
MAYBELLINE
Same as Scene 1

SARA LEE
Same as Scene 1

Scene 4
OVELLA
Same as Scene 1 (keeps corset, etc. underneath)

TEDDY JOE
Same as Scene 1

Scene 5
SARA LEE
Same

BO BOB
Same as Scene 1

Scene 6
MAYBELLINE
Floral peasant, off-the-shoulders blouse
Boa
Black miniskirt
Black net stockings
Platform shoes

OVELLA
Same

SID
Same as Scene 1

Scene 7
CLARENCE
Same (dresses in scene)

TEDDY JOE
Same

Scene 8
SID
Same

MAYBELLINE
Same

BO BOB
Same

Scene 9
SARA LEE
Same

CLARENCE
Wranglers
Western shirt
White undershirt (tank)
Cowboy boots
Cowboy belt

ACT II

Scene 1
SID
Same
Changes western shirts

CLARENCE
Old t-shirt
Old faded Levis
Lace-up work boots

BO BOB
Same

Scene 2
SARA LEE
Same
Changes western shirt
Changes earrings

OVELLA
Sequin silver tube top
Black spandex pants
High black boots
Hot pink scarf (from Scene 1, now used as sash)

Scene 3
CLARENCE
White undershirt (tank)
Same green boxers
Jeans (Maybelline dresses him into)
Work boots (Maybelline dresses him into)

MAYBELLINE
Same waitress uniform
Trenchcoat
Ski hat

Sunglasses
Cowboy boots
(Note: Remove hat, glasses and coat and leave in Lowake Inn)

Scene 4
MAYBELLINE
Same waitress uniform
Same cowboy boots

TEDDY JOE
Three-piece suit
Dress shirt
Tie
Black dress shoes

Scene 5
SID
Same

BO BOB
Same

OVELLA
Old jeans
White T-shirt
Letter jacket
Scarf covering hair
High heels (wears one, carries a broken one)
Pom Pom

Scene 6
SARA LEE
Belted dress blouse
Black stretch pants
High heels
Long earrings

TEDDY JOE
Same

Scene 7
SID
Same
Changes western shirts

BO BOB
Suit
Bolo tie
Dress Shirt
Cowboy boots
Cowboy belt
Cowboy hat

MAYBELLINE
Same

OVELLA
Floral skirt
Pink blouse
Flats
Wig

TEDDY JOE
Same

SARA LEE
Same

CLARENCE
Same as Act I, Scene 9
Changes western shirts

PROPERTY PLOT

BLUEBELL'S
ONSTAGE
Hat rack
    baseball caps (2)
    jeans jacket
    sweater
Small round table w/blue table cloth
Two chairs
Bar
    On top of bar
    small toaster oven
    fried pie rack
    six fried pies
    bowl of popcorn
    chip rack five bags of Fritos
Behind and underneath bar
    six bottle-capped Lone Stars
    six cans of root beer
    six empty Lone Star bottles (pre-set on table before Act II)
    bar manual (sprinkled with powder)
    bar rag
    bottle opener
    bowling bag and ball
    guitar (Sid)
Two bar stools
On wall above bar
    mirror
    Sid's postcard collection
    Texas bumper sticker

Lone Star neon sign
Budweiser neon sign
Beads in doorway to storeroom

OFFSTAGE
By bar's storeroom
  broom
  Sara Lee's red carnations
  feather duster
  pot and pans (for crash SFX when Maybelline does inventory)

LOWAKE INN
ONSTAGE
Bed
  Headboard
  Ugly orange bedspread
  Yellow floral sheets
Bedside tables (2)
  Television
  Gideon's Bible
  Clarence's cigarettes (pre-set Act I, for Scene 2)
  Clarence's lighter (pre-set Act I, for Scene 2)
Yellow curtains
Ugly velvet painting
Mirror

OFFSTAGE
By Front Door
  Shotgun (Teddy Joe)
By Bathroom
  Band-Aids (Teddy Joe)

Two Lone Stars (Teddy Joe)
Bag of trash and empty bottles (pre-set Act II scattered around room for Clarence, Maybelline dream scene)
Bloody white towel (Teddy Joe)
Suitcase (Ovella)
Wig head (Ovella)

OUI COIFFER
ONSTAGE
Beauty station table
    Bobby pins
    Hair spray
    Sara Lee's Virginia Slims
    Sara Lee's lighter
    Ashtray
    Box of Kleenex
    False eyelashes (stick-on type)
    Blue eye shadow
    Blusher
    Hair piece
    Teasing comb
    Cup of water
    Pink lipstick
    Hand mirror
    Magazines on lower shelf
    Dye bottle (for Ovella's "treatment")
    Plastic gloves (for Ovella's "treatment")
    White towel with a snatch of Ovella's hair
Beauty shop chair (foot pump style)
Hair dryer
Knickknack shelf w/misc. knickknacks

BO BOB'S MAIL BAG
  Misc. mail
  Rubber bands
  Cosmo (Sara Lee)
  Playboy (Teddy Joe)
  Anniversay Card

Ring box and ring (Clarence)
Tickets for George Jones concert (2)
Ring box and ring (Bo Bob)

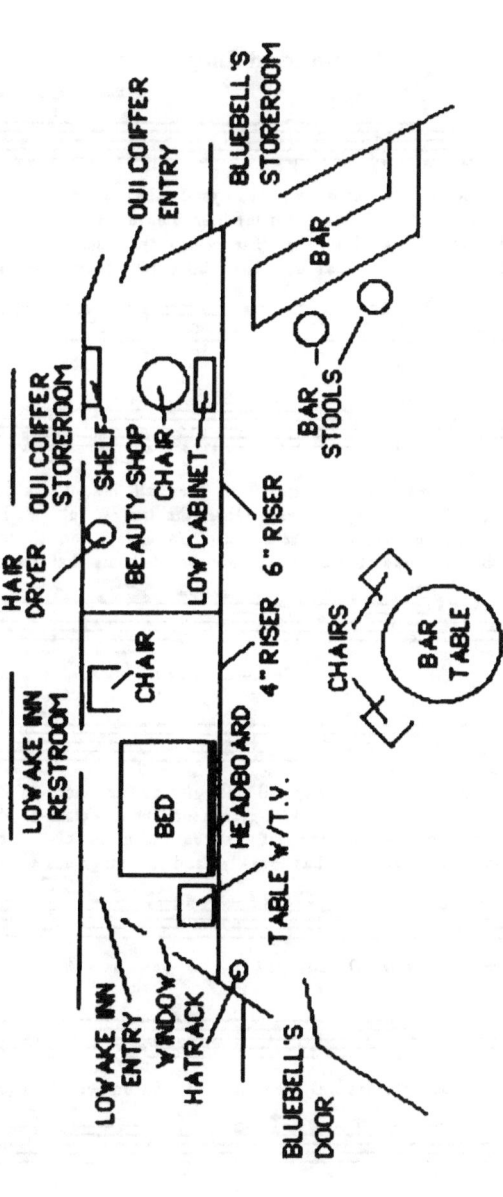

SCENE DESIGN "CHEATIN'"
WILLIAM MAYNARD, DESIGNER

ORIGINAL PRODUCTION, MAINSTAGE PRODUCTION, NORTH HOLLYWOOD, CALIFORNIA

THE OFFICE PLAYS
Two full length plays by Adam Bock

THE RECEPTIONIST
Comedy / 2m., 2f. Interior

At the start of a typical day in the Northeast Office, Beverly deals effortlessly with ringing phones and her colleague's romantic troubles. But the appearance of a charming rep from the Central Office disrupts the friendly routine. And as the true nature of the company's business becomes apparent, The Receptionist raises disquieting, provocative questions about the consequences of complicity with evil.

"...Mr. Bock's poisoned Post-it note of a play."
- *New York Times*

"Bock's intense initial focus on the routine goes to the heart of *The Receptionist's* pointed, painfully timely allegory... elliptical, provocative play..."
- *Time Out New York*

THE THUGS
Comedy / 2m, 6f / Interior

The Obie Award winning dark comedy about work, thunder and the mysterious things that are happening on the 9th floor of a big law firm. When a group of temps try to discover the secrets that lurk in the hidden crevices of their workplace, they realize they would rather believe in gossip and rumors than face dangerous realities.

"Bock starts you off giggling, but leaves you with a chill."
- *Time Out New York*

"... a delightfully paranoid little nightmare that is both more chillingly realistic and pointedly absurd than anything John Grisham ever dreamed up."
- *New York Times*

SAMUELFRENCH.COM

www.ingramcontent.com/pod-product-compliance
Lightning Source LLC
Chambersburg PA
CBHW070645300426
44111CB00013B/2265